BAD BIRTHDAYS

ACKNOWLEDGMENTS

Special thanks to Jeannine Dillon,
Kirsten Hall, Kelly Murphy Bruen, Adrienne O'Hayre,
and, as always, my husband Andrew Fu.

First Published in 2014 by
Hampton Roads Publishing Company, Inc.
Charlottesville, VA 22906
Distributed by Red Wheel/Weiser, LLC
www.redwheelweiser.com

ISBN: 978-1-57174-717-4

Library of Congress Cataloging-in-Publication Data
available on request

Printed by South China Printing Company Ltd

10 9 8 7 6 5 4 3 2 1

BAD BIRTHDAYS

THE TRUTH BEHIND **YOUR** CRAPPY SUN SIGN

SARAH CHRISTENSEN FU

HAMPTON ROADS

INTRODUCTION

My personal relationship with horoscopes and astrology has gone through many stages. As a teenager and college student, I found the study fascinating and oh-so-relevant. I loved learning which tendencies the different signs had, and how the movement of the planets impacted on people's moods and behavior. I studied compatibility reports tirelessly and considered how I would map out my sexual and romantic pursuits.

I had, however, one major problem with astrology. I hated my sign. I was born a freaking Virgo—arguably the most boring, unsexy, lame sign in the entire zodiac.

"But I'm not boring," I argued to myself. "I'm a fascinating, creative, unique person." So I did some more research. I looked at my Moon sign and my rising planets, and by analyzing the exact time and place of my birth I was able to build up some more detail. My new, more complex

horoscope *still* basically said I was just incredibly boring... except it didn't come right out and say that. My chart used euphemisms such as, "reliable," and "dependable," and "doesn't like change," and "total control freak." *Whatever!* I could go with the flow like nobody's business. Couldn't I?

I took a break from astrology for a while. I spent the latter part of my twenties never even using, "What's your sign?" as a pick-up line, let alone as a genuine conversation topic. I carried on with my life, moved to New York City, went to graduate school, had relationships—*lots* of relationships. The one metaphysical allowance I made to myself was to attend the annual Psychic Fair in Denver, Colorado, near my parents' home. Now let's fast-forward to a Fair I went to a few years ago, just before my wedding. So... I'm sitting in the large, open hall with one of the hundreds of psychics and spiritual guides in attendance. Her booth is a card table covered with a lovely, ornate patchwork cloth and a sign on a tripod. A little stack of business cards offering a ten per cent discount sits on the corner of the table. I begin describing my upcoming nuptials, and feel my blood pressure rising. In fact, I feel myself beginning to freak out, and before I know it, I'm walking with the ghosts of boyfriends past, digging through all the past relationships that hurt me.

I blow my nose. (*Yes*, that's right, I was *crying* for some reason at this point... I always get emotional at the Psychic Fair—I think that's a "me" thing, not a Virgo thing.) I go on to explain how my first love, my high school boyfriend, had cheated on me and left me and I was scared that my husband-to-be would do so as well. The psychic crinkles her wise eyes and says, "Oh dear. What sign was he?" I told her that the ex was a Pisces, and that my fiancé is a Leo. She frowned. "Oh dear. Well, you may have issues with the Leo in other areas, but he won't cheat. They're very loyal... But of *course* the Pisces cheated on you. He felt like you didn't and couldn't *really* love him. And you probably really went outside your comfort zone with him, too, to try to make sure he *didn't* cheat on you." I blink a few times. She'd nailed it. She hands me a tissue and I blow my nose—loudly. She holds up

the trashcan and I toss in the wad. She clicks her tongue, "I could have told you that a Virgo-Pisces match would end in infidelity and saved you that pain."

I remember it vividly. At that moment, I wanted to stand up and scream. Why *didn't* anyone tell me, then, if it's such common frikkin' knowledge? Why wasn't there a *book* that told people the *truth* about their signs and their compatibility? After leaving the Psychic Fair I went back home and launched an investigation, just to make sure that I hadn't overlooked something that stated the outright truth about my compatibility (or lack of it) with my ex, and really could have saved me the trouble of wasting time with him. Everywhere I looked I saw that a Virgo-Pisces match was mostly healthy, though everything was so vague! There were broad, sweeping statements like, "Pisces's unreliability may disturb Virgo." Um, yes! For some reason it disturbed me greatly when he was *unreliable...* and slept with other people.

I read and thought more. I brought out old resources that I used to read and checked into other aspects of my zodiac chart. I looked at family relationships, career choices, money. I looked at how I would be as a parent, how I would relate to my friends. And everything I read was double-talk.

"Virgos born on this day care more about their passion for their job than their money." That basically means that I shouldn't expect to get rich. "Virgos born on this day may find that they have different opinions on child-rearing than those of their friends." This one basically means that I would grow up to be a judgmental mommy, right? Well, when the normal wishy-washy zodiac descriptions are boiled down to their essentials, all that's remaining is what stinks... what chip you were born with on your shoulder... which cross you were born to bear. Knowing the good stuff is the icing on your cake; knowing the bad stuff can save both your life and your relationships.

I decided, as I browsed, that all these euphemistic phrases—peppered liberally through the regular zodiac horoscopes—are basically ridiculous. The astrologers who study the skies and delve into nature's impact on human behavior are very astute—but they're too scared to say what they actually *mean*. They think that, if they're general and vague, they will be able to cast a wide enough net to encompass all of the possible relationship outcomes that may play out between two signs.

This is *not* that book. This book is about the worst possible scenarios. This book will tell you outright if your doomed relationship will end in infidelity—and if it's wrong, and your partner doesn't stray... then, hey, you got lucky and ended up with a spouse whose personality defies their zodiac sign. If the astrological descriptions in this book don't apply to you, that's a *good* thing... because this book is filled with the most despicable, disgusting, and aggravating aspects of your star sign.

Through the course of my study, and in writing this book, I have actually come to terms with my Virgoness. My vexatious Virgonity. Now that I'm married and have kids (a Leo and twin Scorpios, Lord help me), I realize that being "reliable" and a "total control freak" suit me just fine. I'm even fine without amassing a large amount of wealth because I have a job that I love (although, if you want to send in donations, just contact my publisher).

The truth is that each sign has its own terrible qualities and its own fatal flaws. Take a look, read ahead... and find out the truth about whether or not your zodiac sign brings out the worst in you.

ARIES generally use force to get their way instead of the itty-bitty bits of brain they have in their head.

TAURUS dislikes change so much that he or she is completely unwilling to listen to a significant other.

GEMINIS are shallow, gossipy, sarcastic, and think that they're better than everyone else.

CANCER comes across as weak. No matter how often they leave the house, deep down they'd much rather be in sweatpants in front of the television.

LEOS are egomaniacs and so non-analytical about their lives that they end up ruining their careers—and personal opportunities for growth—without even realizing it.

VIRGO is such a control freak that all the pleasures of life can fall by the wayside when they are trying to shape their world to meet their very specific needs.

LIBRA is incredibly vain, so much so that trying to have intellectual or deep conversations with them rapidly becomes pointless because they can see only their own point of view.

SCORPIO is basically just mean-spirited. Scorpions are vengeful and if you disobey their wishes, they will find some way to make you regret it.

SAGITTARIANS are foolish, putting their own short-term happiness above anything else.

CAPRICORN has to be right all the time. Capricorn would rather assume that everyone else on planet Earth is brainless than admit to being mistaken about anything.

AQUARIUS is on a soapbox all the time, and is constantly judging others about what they're doing wrong.

PISCES would rather mope impotently and grieve all the things wrong with the world than actually take action to change anything.

This is merely the tip of the astrological iceberg. You'll get a chill down your spine when you find out what it means to be born on your birthday. Read on, my friends, and weep.

TABLE OF CONTENTS

ADVERSE ARIES

MARCH 20 TO APRIL 19

Aries is the boss of it all, or at least the Ram's strut makes it clear that he or she *thinks* they own the joint. What is it about Aries that makes them so confident? Is it their natural-born intellect—um, yeah, no, not so much. Aries, just like the powerful, muscular man-sheep that represents them in the cosmic zodiac, have way more brawn than brains. Their handy horns and blind, dumb ambition open doors for them that they could otherwise never have figured out how to work. Aries will just keep at it, battering down obstacles—left, right, and center—until they meet their goals.

It's not that Aries are sociopaths or anything like that, it's just that they really don't care about other people very deeply. They can still operate within a family unit, and show up to birthday parties and ballet recitals, but the only real charge they get is from locking horns with the world and getting their destiny on track. They want to climb every mountain, ford every stream, find every rainbow... you get the picture. Arians need to find their

11

own way in the world and deeply resent anyone who tries to make things easier for them. If there's a choice between a clear-cut hiking trail and a wooded-over, lesser-traveled path, it's pretty damn obvious which one the Aries is going to take.

Aries, you don't tolerate any social funny-business. If someone uses the word *"can't"* you might literally lose your mind. You rarely put something off, but when you do, it's because you're calculating your plan of attack. When other people put something off, it's because they're complete lazy-asses—and you'll tell them that to their face. You don't have a problem playing the "bad guy" and laying down the law. It seems as though you would not be invited to happy hour very often, but for some reason people like to have you around. Your swagger makes everyone else feel just a tad cooler. Don't be too flattered, though. They all talk about you behind your back.

LOVE AND RELATIONSHIPS WITH ADVERSE ARIES

The best thing you can do to pique an Arian's interest is to act like you're not interested. That's basically the cardinal rule for interacting with an Aries. They love the chase and if you offer yourself up on a silver platter, they will immediately become disinterested. Aries will absolutely let you know exactly how he or she feels about you when the time is right—they are not shy with expressing their feelings and intentions. You have to treat an Aries like a fish on a hook once you capture their interest, letting the line out a little bit and then drawing it back in, then out again, then in again... and then they'll be fully hooked.

Unfortunately, keeping an Aries on the hook once you've caught him or her is a highly physical and exhausting proposition. Aries needs the flames of passion to be consistently blazing—so try to keep things fun, exciting, and adventurous. Otherwise, an Aries may promptly lose interest and seek the heat elsewhere. Loving an Aries is like loving an erupting volcano. You're almost certain that you'll be burned—it's practically a statistical certainty—but it's so thrilling that you have to at least try.

Aries is very competitive, and sees his or her romantic partner as a possession, a prize to be won or lost. If you want to rendezvous with an Aries, you should look the part of a trophy date—nothing will make the Ram prouder than strutting around with a hottie on his or her arm. Conversely, if you aren't at your smokin' hottest, don't expect Aries to roll out the red carpet for you. They will notice when you bring it, and when you'd prefer to be at home in front of the television wearing sweats. Aries is more terrified than other signs of growing old and irrelevant, so if their date admits they'd prefer to be at home watching Netflix, Aries might panic, run out for the evening, and find somebody new to tickle their fancy.

CHECKLIST FOR DATING AN ADVERSE ARIES

You'll need at least half of these things to have a successful relationship with an Adverse Aries.

Sex appeal: Just remember, if it weren't for the promise of regular intimacy and sexual intercourse, Aries would just stay single for ever. In Aries's mind, his or her lover needs to fulfill their part of the bargain by looking—and acting—like their sexual fantasy.

Thick skin: Arians say what's on their mind. They don't sugar-coat it, they don't cushion it, and they certainly don't hold back... and that's when they're in a *good* mood. When they fall into a bad temper, you really need to toughen up. You have to be able to take what they dish out without falling apart, or they will lose their respect for you.

Affection: More than just hooking up, Aries needs to feel like they are important to you. If you find ways to show your affection and appreciation, like surprising him or her with flowers or some light poetry action, Aries will really value your efforts. Just don't err on the side of cheesiness, or Aries will suspect that you're just putting on an act.

Truth: Do not lie to an Aries. Aries will always tell you the truth, and if he or she finds out that you've lied... you're toast. Don't even try to stretch the truth. Don't omit the important facts. Just come to the table naked and honest and be who you really are. Aries will admire that. They may not want to date the "real" you, but they'll at least respect you.

A backbone: Your Aries will argue, insist, and even manipulate to get his or her way. Don't give in. Respect is a cornerstone to a successful relationship with a Ram, and if you are constantly bowing to his or her demands, you'll seem very weak. If you need to, practice saying, "No. Not this time," in the mirror until you're ready to actually try it out on your Aries partner.

Loose reins: Whatever you do, don't try to control Aries. It won't go over well at all. Aries needs to be free and independent to make their own choices, and if you come between them and their passions, you will be the one to get burned.

ADVERSE ARIES COMPATIBILITY

ARIES AND ARIES LOVE

Two Aries together basically makes life a giant competition. Who will be the most romantic? Who will be the dominant lover? Who will be the loser who has to do the dishes? Who will make the most money? Your entire relationship will be spent jockeying for power in every aspect of your life.

ARIES AND TAURUS LOVE

Aries will appreciate Taurus's strength and conviction, and the Ram and Bull will be able to resolve their conflicts when they butt horns. Taurus will slow Aries down and Aries will liven Taurus up. The two will enjoy each other's company in the bedroom and the rest is all details, right?

ARIES AND GEMINI LOVE

After an introductory stage—during which Gemini will overthink and second-guess whether or not dating the passionate, demanding Aries is a good idea—these two will settle into a routine that primarily involves going out to show off and then coming home to connect intimately. Both will be completely satisfied with this routine.

ARIES AND CANCER LOVE

Cancer doesn't mean to be weak, but their natural sensitivity makes Aries want to put on his or her armor and come to the rescue. However, this imbalance of power in the relationship will make Aries resent Cancer, and Cancer will never really feel secure with an Aries for a mate.

ARIES AND LEO LOVE

These lovers bring out the best in each other. Aries is strong enough to be able to encourage Leo's swelling ego, and Leo is hot enough to match Aries's brightly burning flame. The only downside is that their super-hot sensuality comes across as über-*obnoxious* to their friends and family, and this couple may get the hose turned on them from time to time.

ARIES AND VIRGO LOVE

The more Aries looks at Virgo, the more his or her attraction fades away. Sad, but true. Even if Virgo is a good physical match, their desire to spray everything

with Fabreeze and disinfectant is so sexually
diminishing that Aries just has to walk away.

ARIES AND **LIBRA** LOVE

Libra treats Aries like a bedraggled orphan taken off
the streets in a novel by Dickens. A love affair can begin
as Libra is metaphorically combing the tangles out of
the wild Aries's hair and dressing him or her in clean
and respectable clothing. Once Libra falls for Aries,
the couple has a great chance of survival despite the
harshness of the outside world.

ARIES AND **SCORPIO** LOVE

Flip a coin. Heads, you go to bed together and enter
into what is definitely going to be the most gratifying
and tumultuous relationship you've ever had; tails, you
respectfully part ways and get on with your life. The
odds of the coin flip are about the same as the odds of
the relationship working, so this is really the only good
way to figure it out.

ARIES AND **SAGITTARIUS** LOVE

An Aries and Sagittarius union is fun and exciting. This
couple can have a wonderful time without needing to
have "the talk" to define their relationship for a very
long time, but eventually the Ram will want to make
sure the Centaur isn't shooting out arrows all over town.

ARIES AND **CAPRICORN** LOVE

The best example of how two signs' fatal flaws will
clash. If they actually make it through the trip it will be
a miracle, and when they get home and unpack their
furniture, things will come to a head. Capricorn will
insist that there's a set of instructions in there for a

reason, while Aries will be confident in his or her ability to find *a better way* to construct the furniture.

ARIES AND AQUARIUS LOVE

But what does it all *mean*, man? Aries and Aquarius will welcome one another's assertions about the cosmos, the meaning of life, the true nature of love, and all sorts of other lines of philosophical inquiry. Their downfall as a couple will come about because they want to constantly get one up on each other... they should check in with themselves to see just how *friendly* their friendly competitions are.

ARIES AND PISCES LOVE

Pisceans keeps trying to get to know the *real* Aries, way down deep inside. Aries is like, "Sorry, this is it." Pisces doesn't understand that Aries puts everything out on the table and holds nothing back—there are rarely deep, dark secrets that need to be excavated.

CAREER AND MONEY FOR ADVERSE ARIES

Aries's competitiveness can be put to great use in the workplace! If you can channel the aggressive attitude of a Ram, they can do an astounding amount of work. Their high energy keeps them going long after others need to recharge their batteries, and they are often the first ones through the gate on a new project. They love to be the best at everything they do and will actively seek out ways to produce better results than their colleagues. Aries are generally the people who come into work whistling, a full half-hour early, just to get an edge on their coworkers. Each day is a new arena and they can't wait to spill blood and be crowned the victor.

Aries is zealous about knowing the state of the state. He or she will subscribe to industry-specific publications, read up on competitors' blogs, and may be the only ones who read those company-wide newsletters. They consume all this information to get an idea of the Big Picture and ways to improve themselves— in order to be *stronger*. They also read national publications, listen to public radio, and can tell you exactly what's going on in the nation and the world. They are knowledgeable and may even evolve into downright, smug little know-it-alls, but they will take the time to share their information with others on their team.

Aries is a smart, efficient delegator and really likes to be the one who gives out the orders. No one else in the zodiac takes more pleasure from having subordinates to boss around. Conversely, Aries can be uncomfortable if they find themselves getting too much input from their boss, and need to be recognized as the strategic genius they believe themselves to be. If an Aries is unhappy and mistreated in the workplace, they might actively sabotage projects. Their temper and need for control and independence can get the better of them, particularly when they're very young and/or of a particularly low IQ. They can get incredibly frustrated with low-performing colleagues, particularly ones who offer up a host of excuses about why the job isn't done.

To Aries, anyone who says they need time to think something through is ultimately just being lazy. And then, for some reason, people think it's *rude* when Aries tells them to their face that they are lazy, and so quarrels in the workplace may follow an Aries from job to job.

ABSOLUTE WORST JOBS FOR AN ADVERSE ARIES

Outgoing Call Center Employee: This job would bore anyone, but it may drive an Aries to stick pencils into his or her eyes. Ironically, they might actually be quite good at convincing people to buy whatever it is they're selling, but the repetitiveness and the sitting down for eight hours, and that stupid little bell that the boss makes you ring when you get a sale—it would all just be too much for a proud, energy-filled Aries.

Scientist: Aries aren't always very bright, and they're almost never detail-oriented. They could very likely wreck a carefully designed study by their lack of attention. Aries tend to multitask, and their inability to focus on what's right in front of them might literally make their project blow up in their face.

Politician: The problem with an Arian politician is that Rams simply don't lie well. For a politician to be successful, he or she needs to be able to spin the truth in order to capture the most votes. Rarely will an Aries be able to force him- or herself to pander to the population and lower him- or herself to tell an untruth. In the end, if they do lie, they will do it so poorly that they will lose the votes anyway.

JOBS THAT AN ADVERSE ARIES MIGHT NOT SCREW UP

Military Surgeon: Military surgeons have to think fast. They have to be resourceful and precise, and the stakes are very high: it's life or death. This type of professional intensity brings out the best in Aries, and though their survival rates may not be the highest out there—hey, they will sure have a great time doing it.

Small Business Owner: Aries loves to be the boss, and being a small business owner puts him or her in the driver's seat. They have smart ideas and good timing— they know how to strike while the iron's hot. They can juggle the different aspects of small business ownership and the pressure of doing everything themselves will bring out the diamond in an Aries.

Advertising Sales: Picture Aries in a lovely business suit, entertaining clients at a fancy restaurant, wheeling, dealing, and signing big contracts. This type of job is the perfect match for an Aries, and the Ram can easily handle the long hours and tireless work of the industry, and also thrives on the competitive nature of the playing field. Aries also wouldn't mind a job that encouraged drinking with clients and the occasional sexcapade, so it's a win-win all the way around.

STARS OF THE SIGN ADVERSE ARIES

Aries have excelled in nearly every industry; it's challenging to single out the most impressive Rams from the herd. They pepper professional sports both as coaches and as world-class players. Many famous musicians are of this star sign, along with their managers and agents in the music industry. The list of Arian entrepreneurs is perhaps the most impressive. The inventor of the M&M and other delicious candies, Forrest Mars, Sr., is an Aries. The makeup mogul Bobbi Brown is also a Ram, who has combined the Arian love of aesthetics with success in business. Also an Aries... Sam Walton, creator of the American store chains Wal-Mart and Sam's Club, chains that incidentally sell both M&Ms and Bobbi Brown Cosmetics.

British entrepreneur Lord Alan Sugar is an Aries, and has amassed an enormous empire of profit-earning businesses, and Hugh Hefner, creator of the *Playboy* empire has amassed an enormous number of girlfriends. Men's designers Marc Jacobs, Tommy Hilfiger, and Kenneth Cole are all Arians and have created entire lines of clothing, cologne, and home goods bearing their name.

Having one or more Aries on your team is a sure way to propel it forward to success, and that can be seen over and over again. Two of the stars of the *Sex and the City* foursome are Aries gals: Sarah Jessica Parker and Cynthia Nixon. Also, at least two of the classic quad of artists, reincarnated in popular culture as the *Teenage Mutant Ninja Turtles*, are Aries: Leonardo da Vinci and Raphael. It's also possible that Donatello *could* have been an Aries, but no one alive today seems to be totally sure of his actual birthdate.

ADVERSE ARIES BIRTHDAYS

⚡PISCES–ARIES CUSP
If you were born between March 19 and March 23, you fall into the Pisces-Aries cusp and can display traits belonging to both signs. You tend to display the stubbornness of the Ram with the lack of planning demonstrated by the Fish, which basically means you adhere fiercely to your "amazing plan" of having no plan at all.

⚡MARCH 21
A March 21st Aries thinks of him- or herself as a role model to others and will take every opportunity to explain the decisions and the thought-process that led

them there. They consider themselves a success story that others can live up to, but somehow miss everyone rolling their eyes behind their back every time they break out another "life lesson."

⚡ MARCH 22

Your partner is lucky to be with you, right March 22nd-er? I mean, without being rude or cruel, look at you... and then look at him or her. *They won the Love Lotto.* Unfortunately, this type of egotism will probably destroy all your relationships. Fortunately, you're better off without 'em, right? Really, who needs 'em? William Shatner, who played Captain Kirk in the famously nerdy *Star Trek* series, was born on this date and has been married *four* times. So, truly, if you were born on this date, you should never settle for anyone who doesn't recognize how incredibly lucky he or she is.

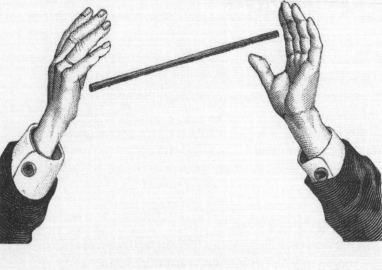

MARCH 23

On March 23, 1755, American Patrick Henry uttered the famous words, "Give me liberty, or give me death," referring to the British rule of the States. An Aries born on March 23 feels much the same way... the open road or a closed coffin. They have a tendency to make declarative, bold, sweeping statements that may come back to bite his or her bottom.

MARCH 24

Magician Harry Houdini was born on this date in 1874. Houdini was an incredibly creative magician, and a master entertainer. March 24th natives also need to pursue creative careers or they'll find themselves stifled, bored, and unproductive. Romantically, they tend to take after Houdini, too, and when they tire of a love affair—*poof*—they simply disappear.

MARCH 25

People born on March 25 are more shy than their Ram brethren, and at social events and family functions they might remain quiet and listen more than they participate. Get a March 25th-er on to a stage, however, and all bets are off. Take famous performers Sir Elton John and Aretha Franklin, for example. They both share this birth date, and while they are understated and underwhelming during one-on-one conversations by many reports, they certainly put on excellent live performances.

MARCH 26

While most Aries rarely know what insecurity means, people born on March 26 live in a perpetual state of terror that they will be found out as frauds. They have always employed the "fake it until you make it" method of self-improvement and have essentially faked themselves into a corner. They often find themselves scrambling to retrace their steps and master essential tasks that they somehow neglected to learn along the way.

⚡ MARCH 27

If it seems like people born on March 27th have egos that are completely out of control, you are *not* crazy. They think that their contribution to the world is truly peerless and they need everyone else to recognize this fact. Two famous divas, Mariah Carey and Fergie of the Black Eyed Peas, were born on this date, and have consistently made headlines with reports of their completely egocentric behavior. While many people find self-affirmations helpful, March 27th natives may need to employ self-*dis*affirmations to avoid infuriating their friends and family.

⚡ MARCH 28

March 28thers change their minds, and jobs, and interests, and hobbies *fast.* One day they're into knitting, the next day they're into sailing. One day they are happy with their job at the bank branch, the next they're bartending at a local watering hole. Pop sensation Lady Gaga was born on this day, and her wild, unpredictable costume changes are a microcosm of the entire life's work for most people who share her birth date.

⚡ MARCH 29

Rams are ordinarily very strong, both mentally and physically, but people born on March 29th may be too emotionally frail and nervous to display the usual Aries power. They worry constantly about being able to live up to the expectations of others and find themselves unable to sleep and sometimes even have a hard time concentrating at work. Arians won't enjoy a particularly competitive career for this reason, and might enjoy working as a life coach, though they may scare away clients by honestly confessing what a stressful mess their own life is.

⚡ MARCH 30

March 30th natives are not particularly choosy when it comes to life mates. They can make do with almost anyone they get along with, so they'll most probably end up hitched to the most convenient option. This is not to say they won't eventually get some loving on the side, and maybe marry multiple times, but as far as long-term commitments go... the easier, the better.

⚡ MARCH 31

The famous French philosopher René Descartes was born on March 31. Along with his famous line, "I think; therefore, I am," Descartes also said, "An optimist may see a light where there is none, but why must the pessimist always run to blow it out?" This kind of thinking is consistent with that of other Arians born on March 31—they hate haters and their optimism and willpower are often the very things that propel them through life.

⚡ APRIL 1

It's hard to admit that you're not where you thought you'd be, isn't it, April 1st-er? You start out full of energy, ecstatically attacking life. You live ferociously, but by the time you look up and take stock of where you are, you haven't gone nearly as far as you'd hoped.

⚡ APRIL 2

Life is no fairy tale for people born on April 2. They struggle with creating meaningful friendships and lasting romances. Hans Christian Andersen, who famously penned the original, ultra-dark stories, now Disney classics, had a tumultuous love life that existed primarily in his imagination. Andersen yearned to connect with love interests that were unattainable, either because they were out of his class—or already married—or because they were men who didn't reciprocate his affections. The famous womanizer Casanova was also born on this date, in 1725, and famously recorded his inability to settle down with a mate in his autobiography.

⚡ APRIL 3

It's not uncommon for someone born on April 3 to think of him- or herself as a real wild child. They probably engage in some risk-taking behavior, sure, but at the end of the day these rebels are just big, blustering teddy bears. Television and movie star Alec Baldwin is an April 3rd native, as was famous stage and movie actor Marlon Brando.

⚡ APRIL 4

April 4th Arians may often describe themselves as Renaissance Men or Women. The truth is... they're not. They can do one, or *maybe* two, things well, and just doggie-paddle through all other aspects of life. Their parents likely tried to build up their self-confidence in areas where they lacked skill and this backfired to make them overly proud of their less-than-stellar achievements in some areas.

⚡ APRIL 5

People may be initially drawn to the earnestness that April 5th natives have, but this admirable honesty can easily turn into a bullying tendency in their personal relationships. The hurt feelings and bruised bonds they leave in the wake of their open communication can destroy their goals of having a pleasant family life and fruitful career.

⚡ APRIL 6

Don't despair if sometimes you look in the mirror and don't see a supermodel staring back at yourself. You have a sexual magnetism and a strong artistic sense, and you will naturally succeed at everything you do. Who needs good looks? Not you.

⚡ APRIL 7

In the film *The Godfather*, goings on within a criminal family help to rocket some people to power and destroy the lives of others. People born on April 7 may find that they're able to succeed only with the help of their friends and family, and if they are alone, they can't seem to meet

any of their goals. Francis Ford Coppola, born on April 7, directed all three movies in *The Godfather* trilogy—so it may be no coincidence that the films focus on those themes. As a side note, be careful not to cross an Aries born on April 7, or you may wind up with a horse's head under your sheets.

⚡ APRIL 8

Like an appetizer that hasn't been fully cooked through, people born on April 8 have an ice-cold center. They are completely focused and choose careers where they can be the best; can compete ruthlessly with others in their field to prove without a doubt that they are superior. Their lack of warmth might be troubling to those around them, but they get the job done, and quite often they are able to bring others up with them as they rise to success.

⚡ APRIL 9

April 9th natives work very hard to make their dreams come true, and they have total faith that they can and will. They are able to break their dreams into actionable steps, and focus on each of these steps until it is successfully completed. *Twilight* actress Kristen Stewart was born on this day, and the growth of her career is no accident. Jenna Jameson, American star of such classic adult films as *Dirt Merchant* and *Zombie Strippers*, shares this birthday—and Jenna's really progressed her career "job by job" as well.

⚡ APRIL 10

It takes a lot of praise to satisfy someone born on April 10. They need to be noticed and rewarded, and if an employer or spouse can give them this recognition, they will never stop reaching for the metaphorical carrot. April 10th natives are incredibly stubborn, even amongst their fellow Aries kin. They don't like change and will be hard-pressed to try new methods of accomplishing things, either at home or in the workplace.

⚡ APRIL 11

Okay, April 11th-er, tell the truth... how many of your friends have you bagged? Probably quite a few of them, because—in your mind—intimacy is intimacy. When you open yourself up to people you know, you naturally feel very attracted to them and aroused by the closeness. Since history has shown that sleeping with people you consider "just friends" is always a good idea and leads to very healthy relationships... by all means, go ahead and keep it up.

⚡ APRIL 12

Intellectually, people born on April 12 stand head and shoulders taller than their Aries peers. High-brow concepts just *click* with people born on this day. They also were born with a sort of super-power—the ability to identify subtle contradictions in others' behavior. Basically, they can sniff out *bullshit* when colleagues or family members serve it up. Sadly, when they call others out on delusions, it can cause major relationship problems.

⚡ APRIL 13

Fictional spy James Bond was born on this day in 1953, when Ian Fleming's first novel *Casino Royale* hit the shelves. Bond, like others born on April 13, can be cold and calculating in his romances. Arians can view romances with the same logic and cunning as they would see business partnerships. And if they feel like they've been double-crossed, they'll put the relationship on ice. Just like Bond, if their partner puts them in a tight spot, they'll give them the slip and find another costar for their next adventure.

⚡ APRIL 14

If you've ever cut your own bangs, you'll know the dangers associated with getting obsessed with things being even. It starts off with a snip on the left side, and then moves over to a chop on the right side, but the right side then gets a little bit too short, so you have to come back around to the left side again. *Et cetera.* People born on April 14 tend to do this with their soul-body connection. They focus a little too much on their soul and completely ignore the physical world, then switch back and lose sight of their spiritual side. It may be good advice to seek out professional intervention—a hairdresser for the bangs and a counselor for the spiritual-physical balance.

APRIL 15

The very first McDonald's restaurant was opened in the United States on this date in 1955. People rejoiced. As history has proven, however, there can be too much of a good thing... and now many people worldwide question the cultural and culinary benefits of a McDonald's. Similarly, spending too much time with someone born on April 15 can adversely affect your mental health. They are stubborn and argumentative and need to be taken in moderation.

APRIL 16

Charlie Chaplin, the famous star of black-and-white movies and master of physical comedy, was born on April 16. He entertained audiences for decades and, in the usual Aries style, he rose to the top of his field through hard work and by taking control of all aspects of his work. Offscreen, Chaplin had significantly fewer laughs. He married three times and was dragged into a very messy paternity suit. Treating romance lightly will come back to bite people born on April 16. They need to sow their oats carefully and choose their partners with serious consideration, or else they may end up paying out all their money to exes and be forced to live like Chaplin's most famous character, "The Tramp."

APRIL 17

Are you particularly clumsy? Many April 17th natives have bruised shins, black-and-blue toenails, and more bumps to the head than they can count. This is primarily because their body and mind are not really in sync. There are some exceptions, however, such as Victoria Beckham, an April 17th-er who has shown the world that she can be at least *slightly* coordinated in executing her dance moves. We'd need to see her shins (without airbrushing) to know for sure if she's got the usual clumsiness associated with this birth date.

⚡APRIL 18

Doctor Who? Oh, *Doctor Who*. The Tenth Doctor in the epic science fiction program was played by David Tennant, an April 18th native. Though Tennant can't *really* travel through time (as far as can be told), sometimes people born on April 18 feel as though they are in some kind of time warp. They see their adult life as a strange reincarnation of their parents' lives, and when they have children this feeling gets even more intense. Egad. Where's the nearest phone booth??

⚡APRIL 19

People born on this date take their financial well-being very seriously. While many other Arians are able to choose between passion and money, April 19th natives are constantly thinking of the family coffers and scrimping in order to amass a sizeable sum. This

can lead to uncomfortable situations with friends at restaurants, where they will find themselves arguing that they oughtn't have to split the bill for the appetizer evenly because *Donna* over there had two extra pieces of cheese bread. After a few instances like this, the April 19th native won't get invited to many restaurant gatherings, so the problem will self-correct eventually.

⚡ APRIL 20

This is a very bad birthday because... well... it's Adolf Hitler's birthday. So, it's pretty much one of the worst birthdays you could have, although most of the time the traits of the Arian people don't come on as strong as they did in Herr Hitler. This terrible day is also marred by one of the first and worst school shootings—the tragedy that took place at the Columbine High School in Colorado. On the positive side, the adorable Woody Allen classic *Annie Hall* was released in theaters on this day, and the chemical element radium was isolated by Marie Curie. It's also a day during which people around the world celebrate marijuana and tend to ingest quite a lot of it. So that's good, too, if you like that sort of thing.

⚡ ARIES–TAURUS CUSP

If you were born between April 19 and April 23, your birthday falls on the Aries-Taurus cusp and you could display characteristics of both signs. You are a combination of the Ram and the Bull, and not necessarily in a good way. You push your way into situations that don't involve you, and try to force your will on everyone else. To lovers and colleagues it sometimes feels like you're trying to parent them, which is really quite obnoxious of you—really, it is.

TRAGIC TAURUS

APRIL 20 TO MAY 20

Tragic Tauruses should be royalty in the Middle Ages. Their idea of a good time is to sit back with a giant, roasted turkey leg and a huge goblet of wine, talk boisterously with friends and family, lounge around in velvet robes, and maybe even get some servant to pop ripe, juicy grapes into his or her mouth. If anyone argues with their decisions, Taurus could just have him or her beheaded on the spot for sport. Unfortunately, there's not much room for royalty in today's technology-based world, so modern-day Tauruses just end up bossing their families around while they sit together at the table eating Kentucky Fried Chicken. The fact remains, however, that Tauruses consider themselves to be the kings and queens of their households and workplaces—*all* ways must be Taurus's way.

Taureans love the physical world around them. They can actually get overwhelmed in places like Yankee Candle or Bath & Body Works. Even Bed Bath & Beyond can be a little too much—who knew towels and bedspreads came in so many textures? They might tear up a little bit when the beauty of an orange-and-blue fall sky hits them full-on. While it can be touching to see the sensitive side of Tragic Taurus, it's usually best to keep them away from very shiny things.

Taurus's fatal flaws stem from their desire to control the things around them. They can have a major temper when they're challenged by their own personal limitations, or by their partner. They will rage against friction and can throw themselves off course with their tantrums. Of course, some Taureans are less assertive than others, and this anger can come in the form of a prolonged silent treatment. Their complete pig-headedness can be a major problem both at home and at work. On top of this, the Tauri people really like to relax, almost to the point of total laziness. While they take pride in doing what they say they're going to do, they may not commit to very many things that interfere with their lounging.

LOVE AND RELATIONSHIPS WITH TRAGIC TAURUS

Tauruses just want to take care of someone. They want to feed and clothe their mate, comfort them and support them. A Taurus is exactly what you want if you're a newborn baby and the Taurus is your parent. If, however, you are a full-grown adult lookin' for hot-n-steamy love, a Taurus might come across as a little bit overbearing and maternal. Can you spice up your

Taurus? Sure you can. Just like you can add chili powder to a chicken breast, or some sort of savory sauce to your tofu, you can encourage a Taurus to be more spontaneous. Just know that settling down with a Taurus probably means twice-weekly sex in the missionary position with the lights out. In the end, though, seeking out a Taurus is totally the right move if you're sick of sleeping your way through the club scene. When it's time to call it quits, go through your little black book and send a flirty text to the least offensive Taurus.

There are things you should know, however, when you get close to that coveted next stage of life with a Taurus. It's very important to a Taurus that they feel in control all the time. They won't tolerate mysterious or fishy behavior from their lover, and if they even perceive the possibility of infidelity, their jealous, angry side will surface. There's nothing more awful to watch than a bullfight, and that's exactly what you'll get if you butt heads with a Taurus. The Bull does not give up easily and, more often than not, they won't even bother to listen attentively to their partner's side of the argument. They are completely inflexible—debating with one is about as useful as debating with a brick wall.

All Taurus wants is to be nice to you, baby, and make your home a nice place to spend time in together. Why do you have to get so many ideas in that little head of yours to interrupt Taurus's flow? Truly, if you can just make yourself a quiet little pet and follow Taurus's instructions, you're in store for some seriously sappy romance. Get ready for heart-shaped coupons on Valentine's Day entitling you to some smokin' sex act (oooh, maybe you can leave the lights on one night if you get a really wild coupon), and thoughtful, expensive holiday gifts. Oh yes, you may get a vacuum cleaner or new underpants, as Tauruses are practical by nature, but look out for an extra little box with something expensive and sentimental waiting on your pillow. Sweet Bull!

CHECKLIST FOR DATING A TRAGIC TAURUS

You'll need at least half of these things in order to have a successful relationship with a Tragic Taurus.

Creativity: You set the stage for romance and—guaranteed—Taurus will play his or her role perfectly. You might need to make cue cards, but a with a little creativity you can definitely grab the Bull by the horns, romantically speaking.

Kid gloves and subtlety: You can catch more flies with honey, or in Taurus's case, you can catch a Bull by avoiding confrontation. If you so much as mention that you notice their flaws and accuse them of being lazy or materialistic (which they obviously are), they could fly off the handle and throw a week-long tantrum. Keep experimenting with gentle ways of delivering your self-improvement hints to the Taurus.

Ambiguity: Face it, most decisions in your relationship are going to go Tragic Taurus's way. It works better if you come to the table with some room for flexibility. If you stop sweating over the small stuff early on, things will go much better for you.

Routine: Taurus really needs to know what they'll be doing at 7:39 a.m. and 2:41 p.m. and all the times in between. Try setting up a shared digital calendar to plan weeks or months ahead. It's an added bonus if you can schedule in time for spontaneous things such as going out for dessert, playing catch at the park, or things that are slightly more naughty and fun.

Good taste: Tauruses love to prepare, serve, and eat a delicious meal. The aromas, the wine, the flavors all melding together—so you need to be able to savor a meal with your Taurus. Put all your concerns about calories and fat on the back burner, and dig in with gusto.

Appreciation of the good life: If for some reason you can't genuinely appreciate everything that Taurus wants to do for you, then just fake it 'til you make it. Eventually you'll get over your self-esteem issues and enjoy actually being treated well for once in your life.

TRAGIC TAURUS COMPATIBILITY

TAURUS AND ARIES LOVE

Confusion may ensue after an immediate burst of attraction. Taurus will wonder why Aries isn't inviting him or her out on formal, candlelit dates. Meanwhile, Aries is just waiting for a firm answer on whether or not Taurus wants to hook up. Hopefully they can stop texting each other evasive messages, overflowing with double-meanings, and just meet up somewhere—somewhere with a well-stocked bar so they can just get over their awkward social dynamic.

TAURUS AND TAURUS LOVE

There's nothing essentially wrong with a Taurus-Taurus match—it can actually be quite comfortable if the two complement one another, personality-wise. However, if the two Bulls bring out the worst in each other, it can be pretty debilitating. They can get lazy fast, and run up their credit cards on material pleasures, just petting one another instead of actively pursuing professional ambitions.

TAURUS AND GEMINI LOVE

Gemini sparkles, and—truthfully—Taurus doesn't even notice. Even if Taurus could see the glimmer radiating from Gemini, he or she wouldn't care. Taurus wants someone easy and dependable to share a life with, and Gemini is anything but easy and dependable. Well... easy, yes. Dependable, not so much. Both deserve a more insightful match.

TAURUS AND CANCER LOVE

Cancer has feelings, and Taurus just doesn't seem to understand that. Cancer can explain how he or she feels for hours on end, using "I-messages," visualization techniques, and metaphors, but—at the end of the day—it's as though Taurus didn't hear a single word that Cancer said. Cancer has very little chance of emotionally manipulating Taurus into changing his or her mind, which makes Cancer feel very sad.

TAURUS AND LEO LOVE

Taurus and Leo can build each other up with compliments and praise. They can also tear each other down quickly and efficiently when they fight, which is often. Neither sign wants to be dominated by the other—the Bull stands up to the Lion at every turn, and the Lion challenges the Bull's decisions, causing irreversible rifts in the relationship and major claw scratches and horn gouges. Ouch.

TAURUS AND VIRGO LOVE

Taurus and Virgo will enjoy this calm and quiet relationship, but all their friends will feel sorry for them. This is the couple that makes budget spreadsheets for fun, and plays *Settlers of Catan* on a Friday night, and embarrasses themselves with totally dated dance moves—like the "lawn mower"—when they drink too much at parties.

TAURUS AND LIBRA LOVE

For this relationship to work, Libra must hide their philosophical and intellectual side and come down to Taurus's level for conversations. Maybe once in a while Taurus will tolerate an abstract conversation about justice, philosophy, literature, or art, but primarily Libra will have to find cultural release elsewhere. A cultural happy ending from a stranger at a bar, perhaps.

TAURUS AND SCORPIO LOVE

To Taurus, Scorpio's mysteriousness might be a deal-breaker. Yeah, the sex is great—really great. Their conversations are good, their goals seem to be in tune, but if Scorpio doesn't explain that fuzzy-bunny suit hanging in the closet, Taurus might lose it.

TAURUS AND **SAGITTARIUS** LOVE

Tragic Taurus would love to keep Sagittarius locked away in a cage, a little songbird to sing just for him or her. Taurus needs to give Sagittarius space in the beginning—probably more space than feels comfortable for Taurus. If Sagittarius lets Taurus get too serious and clip his or her wings too fast, it will mean an unhappy relationship in the long-term, with Sagittarius always questioning what else is out there.

TAURUS AND **CAPRICORN** LOVE

Taurus needs a little more affection than Capricorn can easily give, and the Bull will be left feeling like he or she is not doing enough to attract attention, hugs, and kisses from Capricorn. Capricorn will notice Taurus's flaws very early in the relationship and spend way too much time silently judging Taurus's alien ability to completely relax and tune out the outside world. To Capricorn, this looks like pure, unadulterated laziness. To Taurus, it's simply living the good live.

TAURUS AND **AQUARIUS** LOVE

Aquarius does not understand Taurus's materialism, and might even accuse Taurus of hoarding possessions. Really, why does Taurus need all this crap? This can cause huge problems if not addressed early on. However, since both signs are so stubborn, and so argumentative, if they can actually get past their differences and join forces to work against a common enemy, they can be very successful at steamrolling the opposition.

TAURUS AND **PISCES** LOVE

With Pisces hemorrhaging emotions all over the place, Taurus will just feel like this relationship is a disaster to be cleaned up over and over again. The good—or bad—thing about this union is that Taurus is loyal and stubborn and won't give up on someone they love. So Pisces can basically make a mess of things, and Tragic Taurus will always show up to put back the pieces. Sad, but kind of sweet.

CAREER AND MONEY FOR TRAGIC TAURUS

According to Tragic Taurus, money is what you trade for things you want. And Taurus wants things, all right. A whole lotta things. As a consequence, Taurus needs to find a job that will pay him or her a whole lotta money.

Taurus actually has some pretty impressive skills to bring into the workforce. The Bull is completely reliable—a rock. Their patience and step-by-step approach to every task allow them to complete complex projects in an organized and efficient manner. They approach personal projects the same way, and usually have a checklist prepared for each mundane task. Shake twice, pull up pants, fasten belt, flush, wash, dry. Check.

Tauruses usually don't have pressing, intense professional goals that they must fulfill in order to find happiness in life. They just want to earn a living that keeps them in comfort and style. However, they do have a few rules… Bulls do not like to feel alienated from their labor (note: labor philosopher Karl Marx was, not surprisingly, a Taurus). Taureans want to see the end result and feel the glow of pride from a task successfully accomplished. They will, however, trade a sense of ownership over their projects in exchange for good pay and stability. Stability is of huge importance to a Taurus and without it they will get anxious and argumentative.

Depending on whether you report to or manage a Taurus in the workplace, you might see a very different side of the Bull. The Tauri people tend to manage up, meaning they charm their bosses and let the shit run downhill to their employees. They don't mean to be unfair, but it seems like the most practical approach to the workplace. For any colleague, getting into an argument with a Taurus can end poorly, with everyone losing face, productivity grinding to a halt, feelings being hurt, and the whole nine yards. This should be avoided at all costs.

ABSOLUTE WORST JOBS FOR A TRAGIC TAURUS

Dentist: Tauruses are so sensitive to sights and smells that being a dentist might not be a great fit. The terrible breath, and the nasty, decaying teeth of the general population might cause Taurus to have a total nervous breakdown.

Missionary: "Oh, hello small village in a third world country. I'm here to save you. Wait, where's the five-star hotel and the Egyptian-cotton linen? Where's the food? Most importantly, where is the wine?" For the most part, Tauruses are simply too materialistic to enjoy saving people in very poor parts of the world.

Professional Gambler: Above all else, the Tauri people need stability in their career. They can't handle the uncertainty of an unsteady job such as a professional gambler. They should get a nice, fat government job. But, wait... government jobs aren't so stable anymore either, are they?

JOBS THAT A TRAGIC TAURUS MIGHT NOT SCREW UP

Farmer: The rigid schedule and physical labor of farm work would be perfect for a Taurus, and the blend of home and professional life could create a comfortable mental state for a Bull. Good, clean, dirty work is high up there on a Taurus's list of ideal jobs.

Investment banker: Tauruses "get" money in a way that many other people and signs do not. They can patiently explain financial data and complex concepts while making sound decisions about investments. They also won't feel bad when turning down ridiculous loan applications from people who want to quit their day jobs to become mystery novelists.

Wine or craft beer dealer: The smells, the tastes, the sensuality of wine and/or craft beer is all a complete turn-on to the Tauri people. They can learn about the complexities of the flavor, the process of creating it, the way to pair it with food. The downside is that the Bull might consume all of the stock, so—there's that.

STARS OF THE SIGN
TRAGIC TAURUS

This book would be remiss not to mention the obvious and point out that two of the world's worst dictators and greatest war criminals of all time were born under the sign of the Bull. Representing Taurus's incredibly deep well of pig-headed stubbornness and total inflexibility are Adolf Hitler and Saddam Hussein. Warning: this is what can happen if a Taurus's control freak tendencies are allowed to run wild.

Many famous world rulers, both past and present, are simply full of Bull. Catherine the Great, the famous empress of Russia, was a Taurus, along with Hirohito, the emperor of Japan during and after World War II. More recent Taurus royalty includes Queen Juliana of the Netherlands, who ruled up until 1980, and Queen Elizabeth II, who still holds the throne of the United Kingdom.

Some of the greatest political philosophers—thinkers who changed the world with their ideas— were of the Tauri class. Of course there's Karl Marx, who wrote *The Communist Manifesto* and spurred the communist revolution in both the Soviet Union and the People's Republic of China. Then there's Renaissance writer Niccolò Machiavelli who, in his work *The Prince*, produced friendly little gems like, "It is better to be feared than loved, if you cannot be both," and, "If an injury has to be done to a man it should be so severe that his vengeance need not be feared." Machiavelli and

Marx were both so popular they got an "—ism" added after their names to encapsulate their ideas. Less revolutionary, but no less impactful, the Taurus-born philosophers and logicians that have lived include Søren Kierkegaard, Bertrand Russell, Immanuel Kant, and Kurt Gödel.

Many stars—or Hollywood royalty, if you will—also fall under the sign of the Bull and, for better or worse, they're probably just as important to today's society as the royal and political classes are. The dukes of drama, George Clooney, Al Pacino, and Jack Nicholson, are all Tauruses, along with relative newcomers Robert Pattinson and Channing Tatum. Lady Bulls in showbiz include classic stars Audrey Hepburn and Katharine Hepburn, as well as established, talented beauties Uma Thurman, Michelle Pfeiffer, Cate Blanchett, and Renée Zellweger. Rule on in good faith, O Hollywood Royalty.

TRAGIC TAURUS BIRTHDAYS

⚡ARIES–TAURUS CUSP

People born between April 19 and April 22 are considered to have been born in the Aries-Taurus cusp, and can display characteristics of both signs. So... what do you get when you cross a Ram with a Bull? It's not a good time, that's for sure. The Aries-Taurus combination makes these people especially stubborn and aggressive. People born on these dates will never stop pursuing a goal and they simply can't see when it's time to give up and walk away.

⚡ APRIL 21

People born on April 21 seem to have stepped out of the past. They have very traditional beliefs and mannerisms. They believe in pulling oneself up by one's own bootstraps and working one's way up the corporate ladder by being a Company Man or Woman. Good luck convincing a man born on this day that he should be a stay-at-home dad, or a woman born on this day that she should get some formal school learnin'.

⚡ APRIL 22

Henry VIII, the king famous for beheading his wives, was crowned on this bad day in 1509. April 22nd-ers break from the typical Tauri desire to settle down in love and life—Bulls born on this day genuinely enjoy playing the field. April 22nd natives like the seduction aspect of a new love... the stage that fizzles out as soon as couples begin to wear sweatpants and pass gas around one another. In order to stop an April 22nd-er from beheading your relationship, so to speak, you must keep the mystery and decorum alive as long as possible.

⚡ APRIL 23

People born on April 23 know what they like from an early age. They have very distinct favorite foods, favorite songs, favorite seasons, favorite holidays, *et cetera*. On the flip side, they know exactly what they don't like and simply won't tolerate it in their lives. Whether it's people who talk about money, or theme parties, or anchovies, any run-ins with their most hated people or things will send them into a spiral of irritation and anger. Do not try to convince an April 23rd Taurus that they should tolerate something on their "Dislike" list for the sake of a group. That argument will go nowhere fast.

⚡APRIL 24

In their young adult lives, April 24th natives are smart and dependable and make good decisions, but as soon as they have children the "crazy" switch gets triggered and they become the type of parent that everyone hates. They will hover helicopter-style over their children at the playground, refusing to let their Precious Ones get bumped or bullied, and they'll show up at their kids' school accusing the teachers of singling out their child. When their high school freshman turns in a PhD-quality essay on the American Revolution, everyone can guess that their Taurus parent offered them an eensy-weensy bit of homework help.

⚡APRIL 25

On April 25, 1886, Sigmund Freud opened his practice in Vienna. It was there he gathered his data to support his theories of psychosexual analysis and the Id, the Ego, and the Super Ego. April 25th natives have a tendency to be soul-searchers. They want to know what makes them tick, and also what makes those closest to them tick. They spend a lot of time, like Freud, analyzing their thought patterns and dreams. They usually also have a pretty severe Oedipus or Electra complex and spend their adult lives trying to recreate their childhood, putting themselves into the role of the parent.

⚡APRIL 26

Step away from the bag of potato chips, April 26th-er. You tend to stuff your face with carbs and sugar to calm your nerves, and this can lead to health problems in the long run. Try to find healthy ways to deal with your anxiety and nervous energy that don't involve widening your girth and clogging up your aorta.

⚡APRIL 27

If you were born on April 27, you may find your competitiveness to be a problem in your life. At work, you might take pleasure in outperforming others. At home, you might over-celebrate your checkers victory—much to your children's dismay—and you may or may not have sent your racquetball challengers to the hospital with racquet-sized facial bruises. Anger management can't help you, because it's not anger that spurs you on. It's the sheer joy of winning.

⚡APRIL 28

April 28th natives are so earnest that sometimes you think they're joking. They say completely un-cynical things without a trace of sarcasm, such as, "I like your pants," or "Great idea, Bob." They are refreshing in an era of double-speak. People born on this day want their family life to be straight out of a magazine shoot or an old television show, and they would like to be spared any behind-the-scenes ugliness that it takes to get the picture-perfect look.

⚡APRIL 29

People born on April 28 seek approval more than some of their Tauri brethren do. They have a keen sense for when other people are judging them, and feel like they have to rectify it by persuading opposing parties. While they'll still adhere stubbornly to their original game plan, they won't rest comfortably until people agree that their way is the right way.

⚡APRIL 30

It's not that April 30th natives don't want to be successful—they do! It's just that they don't really want to work that hard to get there. Because they're big risk takers, sometimes their gambles really pay off and they find themselves rolling in dough. When the risks don't pay off, they find themselves laying on the couch eating candy corns in June, reminiscing about when they threw that touchdown pass in a high school football final.

⚡MAY 1

Don't bring drama around a May 1ster. Seriously, step off with anything that is not relevant to family or career, or anything that's over-emotional or frivolous. May 1st natives keep themselves far too busy to engage with theatrics. At home, you'll find them stripping paint or ironing the curtains. At work, you'll find them walking on the factory floor, or going out to the warehouse to make sure each step of the process is being done correctly. They keep it real, and to earn their respect their friends and family should keep their emotions in check and their issues in perspective.

⚡MAY 2

It's probable that people born on this date, if they eat vegetables at all, secretly despise them. They don't want to eat a healthy diet. Deep down, they want cheeseburgers, french fries, and milkshakes for every single meal. If they are athletes, as many May 2nd-ers naturally are, they may recognize the need for a balanced diet and force themselves to eat green things. If they are armchair athletes, however, they are likely to be uncomfortable if they don't figure out a way to get all the nutrients their body needs.

⚡MAY 3

When five-year-olds play together, many times you'll hear direct orders pass between the friends like, "You go over there and say, 'Can't stop the beat,' and then throw the ball to me." When May 3rd Bulls play together, you'll hear the same type of bossiness ensuing. This is Niccolò Machiavelli's birthday, and he was most probably a pretty bossy guy when he hung out with his pals, too.

⚡MAY 4

You are inherently aware of the difference between right and wrong, aren't you, May 4th-er? You have a moral compass that guides your every decision and there really is no gray area for you. To live up to your own values, you often punish yourself for your materialistic desires by denying yourself purchases and even physical pleasures such as comfort, or a decadent meal, or fulfilling sex with your partner. While your partner might think you're off your rocker to not let yourself be sexually satisfied, as long as you continue to get their rocks off, your relationship can survive your bouts of self-chastisement.

⚡MAY 5

May 5th natives can change the world if they can override their desire for security and take the risk to go BIG with their ideas. The pop star Adele shares this birthday with famous cook and author James Beard, and philosophers Karl Marx and Søren Kierkegaard were also born on this day. If you share this birthday as well, it's time to put on your big-kid pants and put away your blankie and get out there into the world. You have a gift to offer the planet, so buck up and get on with it.

MAY 6

It is highly likely that your favorite holiday is Halloween, right, May 6th-er? Because it's your chance to show off your very creepy and dark side without totally terrifying those closest to you. Whether you dress up like a spider's egg sac or a dead prostitute, your costume is always just on the icky side of Halloween-appropriate attire. You let your natural creativity shine out in ways that the public may not always appreciate. Orson Welles, for example, who was born on May 6, duped, creeped out, and infuriated the American people with his broadcast reporting an alien attack on New Jersey in *The War of the Worlds*.

MAY 7

It's really not your fault if a May 7th native is not that into you romantically. They may happily hook up with others, enjoying social interactions and physical exchanges, but they will not take a life partner until they find a true soul mate. Similarly, they may do odd jobs to earn money, but they will not commit to a career until they find "the one" that combines their passion with a way to earn a lot of money. So, if you run across a May 7th Taurus who's a corporate tax attorney or a tobacco lobbyist, it's completely acceptable to hate him or her. They didn't just end up in that career by mistake.

⚡MAY 8

Perfect is boring, and people born on May 8 err on the side of perfection in all aspects of their life. They're not even perfectionists, not in the true sense, because that would imply that they carried out their ideas of perfection to an unhealthy degree. They simply exist in this world as a great friend, a reliable employee, a good son or daughter, a solid spouse, and/or a caring parent. After some PG-13-rated rebellion as a teenager, they settle into reasonable, healthy adult habits. The thing that no one else knows about May 8th-ers—one of the most tragic tales of the Tragic Taurus—is that they have this huge dream that they keep completely to themselves. They may want to sing at the Grand Ole Opry, or write a novel, or become an astronaut, and every so often—when they're feeling melancholy—they'll take this dream out of the mental box they've stored it in and gaze at it longingly. Then they'll rewrap it, carefully, store it back on its shelf, and get on with being perfect.

⚡MAY 9

Most Tauruses make it a practice to avoid drama and unreliable romantic partners so as not to upset their primary life goals of achieving stability and comfort. May 9th-ers shirk this trend and seek out exciting love interests that the rest of the world may see as a terrible bet. But the May 9th-er will stubbornly try to make the relationship work until—at some point—they are forced to choose between their career and their lover. Then, they'll almost always stick with their Taurus roots and choose stability in their career.

⚡MAY 10

On May 10, 1924, J. Edgar Hoover started up the U.S.'s Federal Bureau of Investigation. Just like Hoover, May 10th natives tend to be suspicious by nature. They want to believe that people are doing the right thing, but don't really believe it until they see it for themselves. They might do things like show up at their lover's workplace—unannounced—just to say hello, or check up on their child at a sleepover, or put spyware on their family's computers. If you're trying to keep a secret from a May 10th Taurus, let them stumble upon a lesser secret and confess openly to it. This should throw them completely off the scent and prevent them from sniffing out your dirtier crimes.

⚡MAY 11

People born on May 11 tend to have a really explosive temper. They can go from zero to screaming in seconds flat, and when these Bulls see red, they refuse to be talked down. Socially, they want to be surrounded by only the most illustrious people, and they can be critical of even lifelong friends who they see as hacks or frauds.

⚡ MAY 12

Many famous people were born on May 12, from entrepreneurs to writers to comedians. These are people who can rally their resources and make their dreams come true if they have financial support from friends and family, at least when their careers are in their early stages. It's not so hard to soar if you know you can't fall flat, right, May 12th-er? Funnyman George Carlin, born on May 12, once said, "Some people see things that are and ask, Why? Some people dream of things that never were and ask, Why not? Some people have to go to work and don't have time for all that." In this simple joke you'll find the split between the May 12th natives that make it big and the May 12th natives that only scrape by.

⚡ MAY 13

People born on this day can be hyper-charismatic and persuasive. They entertain, preach, propagandize, and basically seduce everyone they meet. Cult leader Jim Jones was born on this date, and he alluringly convinced over nine hundred Americans to join his cult, give up all their possessions, abandon their families, move to Guyana, Africa, and then drink poisonous Kool-Aid in a mass suicide. Actor Stephen Colbert, of The Colbert Report, was also born on this day and, while Colbert is pretty influential, it would be nearly impossible to beat Jim Jones's power of persuasion. Just because you've got a tough act to follow doesn't mean you shouldn't try, though, May 13th-er.

⚡ MAY 14

Stubbornness is a trait that all Taureans share, but May 14th natives tend to turn that stubborn nature on themselves. They judge themselves harshly and hold themselves to totally inflexible and incredibly high standards. They don't feel good about their labor until the world validates the work they do. If they're not getting enough attention at the office, they may awkwardly try to slide their work achievements into conversations at social gatherings. Side note: Mark Zuckerberg was born on this day, so please "Like" and "Share" this on Facebook to show him he's not alone in his awkwardness.

⚡ MAY 15

May 15th natives are just enormously hungry most of the time and feel essentially like a bottomless pit. If you were born on this day and have a slim figure, you probably feel that deep down inside you're just a deprived overweight person. Don't let down your guard or all your hard work will disappear faster than you can say, "Pass the cheese sauce."

⚡ MAY 16

May 16th-ers are lucky. They get to experience the full roller coaster of love, the highest of the highs and the lowest of the lows. It seems like no matter how much they try to stabilize their relationship, the vacillating continues. Their stubbornness and refusal to compromise plays a part in their relationship drama, but their misery primarily comes down to the fact that they secretly love to argue and get a lot of pleasure out of sparring.

⚡ MAY 17

You look tired, May 17th-er. Is it because you're out there, killing it, pursuing excellence like you do every day, or maybe you're coming down with a little something? People born on this day are not show-offs, but they should be, because they are head and shoulders above other people in both their persistence and intelligence. Unfortunately, they worry too much about their health and can be total hypochondriacs. This can slow them down professionally and hurt them socially.

⚡ MAY 18

It's possible that a single, bad break-up has ruined the entire romantic life of a May 18th native. If they seem distant and slightly judgmental when you sidle up to them, it could be because someone a long time ago (or yesterday, for that matter) stomped all over their heart. It could also be because you have broccoli stuck between your teeth... but it's probably the broken heart thing.

⚡ MAY 19

On this day in 1962, Marilyn Monroe sang her famous version of "Happy Birthday" to John F. Kennedy. It wasn't actually his birthday... Marilyn never was very good with dates unlike people born on May 19, who tend to be very good at keeping their calendars. Anyway, the point is that just like Marilyn adapted a classic tune in order to present it in a distinctive way, people born on May 19 also adapt the commonplace to meet their own unique needs. May 19th-ers are the original DIY-ers, and will figure out how to turn a mini-fridge into a Kegerator, or snip and sew to transform hideous curtains into a slightly less hideous dress. They will custom-fit anything, regardless of whether or not it's a wise idea.

⚡ MAY 20

So, somebody once told you that you wouldn't amount to anything when you were a kid, May 20th-er. So what. Shake off whatever that teacher or preacher or troop leader said to you, and dust off your dreams. Sure, you might fall flat on your face if you try to compete, but then again... you might not. The truth is, you will have no idea if you have what it takes to make your dreams come true until you admit that you actually have dreams.

⚡ TAURUS–GEMINI CUSP

People born between May 19 and May 22 are born in the Taurus-Gemini cusp. These people display traits of both signs. In the case of the Taurus-Gemini cusp, the signs share many traits in common. First, both signs love to eat, drink, and get it on, so people born during this time period can find themselves held hostage by their desires for these physical pleasures. Try to get on an every-other-day drinking-and-screwing schedule so that you can channel your boundless energy into more productive and creative activities.

61

DEGENERATE GEMINI
MAY 21 TO JUNE 21

In the zodiac, Geminis are represented by twins. The twins symbolize their dual nature, their dexterity to change modes quickly, and their ability to hold multiple sets of morals and ideals to be simultaneously true. We could stop this chapter here, because this establishes the baseline truth about Geminis: they're two-faced. They'll say one thing to your face, and as soon as they're with someone else, they'll bust out with a completely different opinion. They don't hesitate to flip-flop in their friendships, their politics, or their morals. If you want to be constantly surprised, befriend a Gemini. You never know what they're going to say or do.

Geminis also can't shut up. They think a lot, and they speak a lot, but unfortunately for the rest of humanity, they don't always do it in the correct order. Geminis have to talk through ideas to understand them more thoroughly, and they love to bounce ideas off other people as they're developing them. This means that at least half of what comes out of their mouth consists of completely unformed ideas, or—in layman's terms—verbal diarrhea. Geminis gravitate to others who speak their minds, even if their ideas vary from what is currently considered to be socially acceptable. They also read everything they can get their hands on and like to work their well-read nature into conversations, to prove that they aren't as bird-brained as some of their conversations would lead onlookers to believe.

Because of their dual nature and their social behavior, Geminis find themselves surrounded by a large and diverse group of friends. If you're ever invited to a Gemini's party, assume that you're going to positively detest at least a third of the people there. If you ever casually mention to a Gemini that their friends are scumbags, they'll just laugh it off and say something infuriating like, "It takes all kinds, doesn't it, chap?" Geminis love the thrill of taking risks, even when that means associating with less desirable social circles.

LOVE AND RELATIONSHIPS WITH DEGENERATE GEMINI

There's a statistic floating around out there that something like a third of people regularly cheat on their spouse. Well, Gemini probably inflates that data a bit because it's likely that the vast majority of Geminis have cheated or will cheat. Sorry to be the bearer of bad news, but if you're looking to settle down with a Gemini... there won't be much settling involved. You'll have to constantly keep on your toes to avoid falling into a boring rut. The rut is what will drive Gemini into the arms of someone they see as more exciting, more fulfilling, and smarter than you are. The best way to keep your Gemini engaged is to surprise him or her with new topics of conversation. That might mean going to see movies regularly, constantly reading up on world events, or renting really bad '80s porn to make fun of together—whatever you do, make sure it's new, exciting, and intellectually stimulating. Either that, or you could just become comfortable with a see-no-evil, open-marriage approach.

Speaking of porn, Geminis tend to have diverse sexual interests and a rich fantasy life. If you're not into trying new things, or even discussing new things, a Gemini might not be the right match to bring home to Mom. You don't have to actually dress up in a latex bunny suit to date a Gemini, but you do have to be able to *talk* about dressing up in a latex bunny suit, and let the Gemini explore his or her fantasy orally—er, verbally. Geminis have a great deal of trust in their relationships and will openly share their innermost desires with their partner, but if they're mocked or shamed for their fantasies, they may never share them again. Be very careful with a Gemini's trust because once it's violated, it's almost impossible to regain.

Geminis tend to talk all the time. Half the time, they are not speaking to make a point, but rather just letting ideas burst and flow from their mouth indiscriminately. You might be shocked to hear them switch sides without warning and argue the opposite side in a debate they've had before. They're not exactly changing their minds, they're just exploring the other side of the argument and thinking things through. Sometimes they sound like idiots, but they don't care. To them, speaking is just another form of thinking, and they wouldn't dream of censoring themselves for such silly reasons as consistency and integrity.

CHECKLIST FOR DATING A DEGENERATE GEMINI

You'll need at least half of these things to have a successful relationship with a Degenerate Gemini.

Independence: Or the illusion of independence. If you get all clingy with a Gemini, they will jump through windows, break through walls, and basically do anything necessary to escape. Smothering a Gemini will turn them off faster than any other transgression.

At least one impulsive bone in your body: Geminis change their minds so quickly that one minute you'll be heading to dinner and the next minute they'll want to go to a movie, and then they'll remember that a friend of theirs is playing a heavy-metal gig across town. You'll need to grit your teeth and just go along with the ride in order to feel like you're not depriving your Gemini date of a fun time. Even once you seal the deal and settle down with a Gemini, you'll need to maintain this ability to go with the flow, because if you start restricting Gemini, he or she will find excitement *outside* your relationship faster than you can say, "Let's just stay in and watch a movie tonight."

Mental multitasking: Geminis never stop talking, unless you've made them angry and they're giving you the silent treatment, which is not a good sign. You need to be able to listen effectively, nodding and interjecting where appropriate, while also handling other tasks. This will maintain your productivity and keep your *Chatty Cathy* partner feeling acknowledged and appreciated.

A sense of humor: Geminis really want people to laugh at their jokes, and find them incredibly witty and amusing. If you can giggle, chuckle, and guffaw your way through a date with a Gemini, you're almost certain to get another date.

Opinions: It does not matter if your opinions are consistent, but you need to be able to talk about social and political happenings, about cultural events, movies and books, about history and sports. Geminis have a wide range of interests and they'll want to talk to you about all of them.

A brain: Geminis can be very physical, but their attention won't last long if you don't have brains to go with your bod. They need the whole package in order to remain interested longer than a few hot minutes.

DEGENERATE GEMINI COMPATIBILITY

GEMINI AND ARIES LOVE

In general, relationships with Geminis can either be really good or really bad, depending on the personal traits of their romantic partner. The joining of an Aries and a Gemini is an extreme example of this. For example, if Aries can control his or her temper and just laugh it off when Gemini flirts with the whole town, they could laugh it off together. If Gemini can act supportive and get behind Aries when he or she impulsively jumps into a new business venture and invests all the couple's money, the relationship might last.

GEMINI AND TAURUS LOVE

Taurus, you better step off. You don't *own* Gemini. Gemini ain't your *property.* Taurus may never get it through his or her thick skull that you can't take a wild Gemini and lock it in a cage. Gemini knows why the caged bird sings, and his or her constant singing, talking, chirping, and bleating will drive the sedate Taurus out of his or her mind. Chances are this relationship will never get serious enough to end in divorce, but the only way it will ever really succeed is if Gemini teaches Taurus to loosen up, and if Taurus teaches Gemini to shut the Hell up.

GEMINI AND GEMINI LOVE

The good news is that two Geminis will never run out of things to talk about. They'll gossip, analyze, debate, and argue until the rooster crows. The bad news is that they might give one another whiplash from one another's reversals, about-faces, and changes of pace. "Twins times two" basically means the relationship practically has to support four different sets of desires, and Gemini's short-attention-span-times-two means that the couple might end up with a devastating make-up-break-up dynamic.

GEMINI AND CANCER LOVE

Cancer isn't always great at communicating, and communicating is *all* that Gemini seems to want to do. While Gemini's running their mouth, Cancer is preparing a romantic dinner, lighting candles, and choosing just the right mood music. Unfortunately, it's unlikely that Gemini will slow down long enough to notice. Cancer wants to stay home; Gemini wants to go out. Cancer wants to talk about feelings; but Gemini just wants to get flirty.

GEMINI AND LEO LOVE

It's inadvisable for Gemini and Leo to go into business together, although hopping into the sack together is *highly* advisable. The sex will be terrific. However, between Leo's overblown ego and Gemini's optimism, they'll be unable to recognize and solve the problems that come up with their finances. They will have a good time, though, if Leo can hold back from bossing Gemini around and Gemini can deal with Leo's drama-queen approach to problem solving.

GEMINI AND VIRGO LOVE

It will happen fast. Gemini will be just chatting, as usual, maybe playing devil's advocate about footie pajamas, or debating the pros and cons of peanut butter brands, and suddenly Virgo will get *real.* Virgo will try to call Gemini out on how he or she *just* said the opposite, or point out how the logic that Gemini is using has major flaws. Gemini may recover smoothly from Virgo's verbal lashing, but he or she will feel deeply bruised by the intellectual attack. If this happens too many times, Gemini will simply stop talking to Virgo completely—which means that Gemini will be talking to someone else, if you catch the meaning.

GEMINI AND **LIBRA** LOVE

Geminis and Libras can work out well, especially if they're very wealthy. If they can take their yacht up the riviera and stop at the Musée d'Osay to appreciate the Renaissance-era paintings and sculptures, and discuss the themes over a glass of fine wine, while deciding where to shop the next day for the newest fashions, they will live in bliss. If, however, they're part of the ninety-nine percent, they might find themselves in financial trouble, arguing often about money and growing apart over time.

GEMINI AND **SCORPIO** LOVE

Gemini and Scorpio can succeed if they treat their love affair like they're preparing a delicious, gourmet meal. They have to carefully monitor the temperature to make sure their emotions don't boil over, and treat their partner with care and tenderness, like expensive, prized ingredients. They need to focus on making their presentation of ideas and opinions as thoughtful as the presentation of each course at a fancy restaurant. If they're not willing to put the time into their partnership, they'll end up in the relationship equivalent of a Number Four with fries—scarfed down, balled up, and thrown in the garbage.

GEMINI AND **SAGITTARIUS** LOVE

These two signs make a really strong match, which could be made even stronger by engaging in frisky, open sexuality. These lovers would very much enjoy bringing new people into their bedroom and may want to consider sustaining a polyamorous or even a polygamous relationship. The lady of the relationship could have sister-wives, which would allow for her to enjoy a tight social circle—both Gemini and Sagittarius value close, deep friendships. The male of the relationship could have a variety of sexual partners, which any Gemini or Sagittarius would appreciate. It's win-win-win.

GEMINI AND CAPRICORN LOVE

If these two stay together it's because they are both too stubborn to walk away from a challenge. They are different in almost every way, and not in a good, quirky, complementary rom-com way. Capricorn literally wants to rain on Gemini's parade, and Gemini will pour one hundred percent of his or her energy into teaching Capricorn that rules are meant to be broken.

GEMINI AND AQUARIUS LOVE

When a Gemini and an Aquarius come together, it is certain that they will throw great parties. Not boring old run-of-the-mill dinner parties, but fabulous, memorable parties that will be reminisced about decades later; parties where all sorts of different types of people will come together and have thrilling conversation and really connect on a *deeper* level. Parties where burgeoning couples will make out for the first time, where the cops are called at least once, and where something catches fire... When the party's over, this couple can run into problems if Aquarius is too much of a control-freak.

GEMINI AND PISCES LOVE

Pisces, take heed. Gemini will hurt you. Gemini just doesn't think before he or she speaks, and this can end with Pisces locked in the bathroom crying... again. Pisces will have to grow some thicker skin in order to have a successful relationship with Gemini. The two are in for many late-night, coffee-fueled conversations that explore their dreams and goals and futures.

CAREER AND MONEY FOR DEGENERATE GEMINI

If Gemini has to work in a job that doesn't require brain power, he or she might go postal. They need a career where they can be thoughtful, fast-paced, and where they can problem-solve. They also need a lot of kudos for their hard work, or else they'll get depressed. Geminis are not ones to treat their job like a nine-to-five—instead, they're always plugged in, always checking their email, returning calls and texting. While they're at the office, they're most likely to be found at the water cooler or surfing Facebook. To them, this is genuine networking, not just idle chit-chat, and they're surprisingly successful at harvesting social media "Likes" and turning them into actionable business ideas.

Geminis can write and they can talk, therefore they should be in a career that is communication-based. Since many Geminis see the truth as a moving target, they can be very successful in the field of advertising and marketing. They can also use their silver tongue to argue their points in front of a jury as an attorney. Whatever Gemini chooses, they should plan to change their mind several times over the course of their career. If you are the parent of a Gemini, you should start saving a *lot* of money for college, because it most likely won't be a straightforward career path.

The worst possible place for a Gemini is a job where no one listens to their ideas. Geminis need to be heard and acknowledged for their ideas, and see those ideas implemented. If they aren't challenged in the workplace, or at least entertained, their boredom will equate to low productivity and frustrated management. Bored Gemini might even use their extra time to dig around and ask questions about your business model, because they can be very, very nosey. They will eventually unearth even the best-hidden, seedy schemes.

ABSOLUTE WORST JOBS FOR A DEGENERATE GEMINI

At-home medical billing: Geminis don't even want to read their own bills that they get in the mail, let alone create a career around billing others. They don't have the detail-focus to succeed in a repetitive, highly detailed career and their boredom will result in low productivity. Since Geminis are thinkers, they would be forced to get to the bottom of some of the mysteries of medical billing, and delving into the details and inner-workings of the healthcare system is enough to drive anyone completely batty.

Bank teller: They honestly should not be trusted with their own finances, and absolutely should not be in a position to handle other people's. It is also torture for a Gemini to have to cut their conversations short. While they'd enjoy talking to many different types of people each day, their goal would be to serve as many customers as possible. Launching into thorough conversations with every person who walked up to their window could really get them into trouble. They're also not that great with stress, and if the bank was ever robbed, they would almost definitely freak out and get everyone shot.

Small business owner: All work and no play does not a fun Gemini make. Small business owners have to put everything behind their goals and burn the midnight oil in order to make their dreams a reality. A Gemini could quickly get burned out and run out of creative ideas if he or she doesn't have a chance to relax and socialize. Whether he or she is a franchise owner of a mini-mart or a crafter with an Etsy store, the Gemini will need a partner and a full-on support team in order to make a small business profitable.

JOBS THAT A DEGENERATE GEMINI MIGHT NOT SCREW UP

Tour guide: Geminis know all the dirt on everybody. They have an unbelievable retention rate for gossip, and will be able to spin wild stories around even the dullest geographical locations. They'll research tirelessly and thoughtfully put together a narrative that makes any tour truly come alive. Whether you're creating a visitors' tour for your string-cheese factory or a neighborhood walking tour of superior desert shrubbery, a Gemini is hands-down the right hire for this gig.

Stand-up comedian: Geminis can be really funny and sharp-witted, with impeccable timing. They also can read a crowd and think on their feet to make each show the best that it can be. The Gemini charisma and charm allow them to handle hecklers, and their two-faced nature and sometimes-dark fantasy life can give them plenty of good material to trash all sorts of people.

Bartender/hairdresser: Geminis are natural born talkers. Almost any other astrological sign would dread going to a job where everybody unloaded their personal problems, but Geminis adore that sort of interaction. They will listen to how your wife did you wrong, and about the gossip at your office, and then they'll tell you about how their sister is an idiot and their dog is currently seeing a pet psychiatrist. Geminis can make a wonderful living in a career where chatting others up is their main job description.

STARS OF THE SIGN DEGENERATE GEMINI

An inordinate amount of Geminis are straight-up sex symbols. Johnny Depp, Marilyn Monroe, Colin Farrell, Heidi Klum, and Angelina Jolie are all Geminis—plus Mary-Kate and Ashley Olsen, who sadly may no longer be sex symbols now that they've reached their grown-up status. These very good-looking men and women are able to flaunt their wares for the camera. Geminis can be very erotic, and that red-hot core translates through the camera's lens and straight into the groins of fans across the globe. This star quality is unique to Geminis—no other sign boasts quite as much raw sexuality.

Geminis are useful outside of the bedroom, too. They excel as musicians and athletes, proving that Geminis are able to tap into their talents, work hard, and nurture their craft. In the sports arena, world-class ballers Carmelo Anthony, Nate Robinson, and Allen Iverson were all born under the sign of the Twins, as were tennis stars Venus Williams and Anna Kournikova. Classic musicians Paul McCartney, Prince, and Bob Dylan are Geminis, along with composers Miles Davis and Danny Elfman.

The dark side of the Gemini Twins can come out, though, and commit some truly heinous crimes. If Geminis don't keep their mental health in check, they could unravel quickly and take a lot of innocent people down with them. Ted Kaczynski, the Unabomber, is a Gemini, along with an absurd number of serial killers including David Berkowiz (the Son of Sam), Jeffrey Dahmer (head-in-the-freezer guy), Danny Rolling (the Gainesville Ripper), and Richard Chase (the Vampire of Sacramento). Wait, does the FBI know how high the chances are that the mass murderer they're looking for is a Gemini? They must, right? Right?!

DEGENERATE GEMINI BIRTHDAYS

⚡ GEMINI–TAURUS CUSP

People born between April 19 and May 23 fall into the Gemini-Taurus cusp. While Taurus has a physical, hands-on approach to the world, Gemini is full of ideas and conversations. The Taurus-Gemini blend can be great, resulting in someone who can communicate their ideas *and* turn those ideas into reality. The combo can also be really terrible, resulting in someone who acts before they think, someone who shoots before they ask questions.

⚡ MAY 21

Gemini Twins can be multi-faceted, but people born on May 21 have a seriously dark side. May 21st native Dante, the thirteenth-century scholar and author of *The Inferno* gave into his dark side when he wrote about the horrors of Hell. Jeffrey Dahmer, also born on this date, stalked and murdered young boys and men. Then there was Mr. T., who mercilessly beat up all those who "Jibba Jabba'd" on his clock. If May 21 is your birthday, you probably also struggle with keeping your darker side in check—when you open up to others, they just don't seem to understand your off-beat fantasies and desires.

⚡ MAY 22

On May 22, 1958, rock star Jerry Lee Lewis landed in London for a tour with his new bride. She was thirteen years old. Wait, there's more... she was also his first cousin once removed. This was not so good for his career. Just as family and love were complicated for Jerry Lee and Myra Gail Lewis, Geminis born on May 22 find their relationships to be difficult to navigate at times. They tend to have traditional family values, but find those difficult to reconcile with their view of themselves as exciting and charismatic.

⚡ MAY 23

May 23rd natives are competitive and fun-loving. They are very flirtatious and are likely to have amassed a solid number of notches on their bedposts before settling down to marriage. They love competition in the romantic arena and may seek out people who are in relationships to pursue as sport. When they have children, they also compete with them in sports or with intellectual sparring. Warning: they may become highly agitated when the student overtakes the master, which will eventually happen.

⚡ MAY 24

May 24th natives have a regal presence, and seem to tolerate and even enjoy others' opinions before dismissing any conflicting viewpoints. Their real problem is the conflicting viewpoints within their own psyche. People born on this day always seem to have something gnawing at them; some inner battle that they can't diffuse enough to find peace. Some great musicians with complicated personal lives were born on May 24, including Bob Dylan, Roseanne Cash, and Patti LaBelle.

⚡ MAY 25

Stop fidgeting! If you were born on May 25, you have some sort of nervous tic. It might be bouncing your knee, or touching your hair, but every time you feel uncomfortable, the tic shows up. You're usually able to hide your fidgets from others, but you are always able to feel the heat when nervous energy takes over. Your tic always shows up when someone corners you into conversations about the status of your relationship. Nothing makes you more uncomfortable than definitively declaring how you feel about someone else.

⚡ MAY 26

All your friends told you that the guy or girl you were seeing was *not* good for you. And yet, day after day, week after week, you kept pursuing the relationship. If you're seriously involved with someone, and your friends don't approve... chances are your friends are right. People born on May 26 tend to be drawn to people who will hurt them or treat them unfairly, and only the strongest can resist the Siren song of a tumultuous relationship.

⚡ MAY 27

There's generous, and there's reckless. Boy, do you walk the line. Money burns through May 27th-ers' pockets. No matter how much they earn, they end up spending too much, and their main expense is other people's affections. Their spending knows no bounds when it comes to buying love, whether it be via a round of drinks at the bar, or expensive, unique gifts for special occasions. People born on this day lose interest when a relationship comes too easy, and will often choose the pursuit of new sexual acquisitions over the long-term stability of a life partner. These Geminis really embody the two-faced nature of the Twins. Don't trust 'em, they're all smoke and mirrors and shiny things.

⚡ MAY 28

Spending time with someone who has no fear of failure is unnerving. While their confidence and optimism can be intoxicating, sometimes it can be upsetting that they refuse to see the consequences of their actions. May 28th natives are like this, blithely skipping along the tightrope of life. While you may want to be there to cheer them on, you sure don't want to be there when they metaphorically splat all over the sidewalk.

⚡ MAY 29

John F. Kennedy, born on May 29, is the poster child for this birth date. Good looking, charismatic, amorous, risk-taking, with the ability to be unbelievably convincing. Most May 29th natives do not have a Jackie *and* a Marilyn, but many will have admirers wherever they go.

One of the worst qualities of people born on this date is their naïve belief that they can teach themselves almost any skill or technique through a little bit of research. These are the people who end up in the Emergency Room after trying to rewire their homes themselves after watching a few YouTube videos, or who have to call the city authorities to help round up their chickens because the homemade pen they built has lost its structural integrity. Or, as in JFK's case, they'll get assassinated by a second gunman on the grassy knoll in a mob .

MAY 30

If you were born on May 30, almost every single New Year's Eve you've written down resolutions. Almost every single year, they've included "Lose weight," or "Be healthier," or "Exercise more," or the like. And most probably, every year, by January 10 or so, you've completely abandoned these goals and gone back to your old routines. You're not lazy, but the lack of an organized effort keeps your spare tire full. If you drink, that's probably your primary problem. Too much beer, wine, or booze takes a toll on your waistline and your ability to follow through with your good intentions. Lay off the hooch!

MAY 31

May 31st natives have woken up to their share of rough mornings. They love to go out and have a good time, love to come back home and let the party continue, and in the morning—the second they wipe the sleep out of their eyes—they're ready to get up and do it all over again. If you try to keep up with a May 31st-er, you will find yourself worn down and exhausted in no time.

Many famous people were born on May 31st, and their success is primarily due to their ability to pour their desire for excitement into their career—instead of into a shot glass. Director Clint Eastwood and football star Joe Namath share this birthday, as do actors Colin Farrell and Brooke Shields.

⚡ JUNE 1

June 1st natives are often shocked by the huge gap between the fantasy of a certain life goal, versus the reality. For example, they may say they want to be marine biologists, but when they find out how much education and hard work is involved in that job, they give up working toward that goal. Or, if they jump through all the hoops to meet their target career, they may find themselves dissatisfied with the dull, day-to-day reality of it. Rather than adjust their goals to be more realistic or more nuanced, they just think of themselves as failures.

⚡ JUNE 2

If you were born on June 2, and you don't already have children, you should think long and hard about whether you want to reproduce. June 2 yields people who will helicopter-hover over their children, yammering non-stop in the typical Gemini fashion. They will be the parents at the playground who scold other people's children for playing too roughly around their Precious Little One, and who show up at preschool each week to talk about Junior's progress in sorting shapes and colors. These children, of course, will be traumatized and grow up to be serial killers... or lawyers.

⚡ JUNE 3

June 3rd natives feel like they grew up differently from everyone else. They see the circumstances of their childhood as unusual, extreme, and usually damaging. This makes them feel separate from everyone else, and causes them to jump to conclusions about other people's goals and intentions. People born on June 3 have reasonably good health *despite* everything naughty they do to thwart it, and while they will work hard to pursue their own interests, they will rarely jump in to support someone else's goal.

⚡ JUNE 4

On June 4, in the year 1919, the 19th Amendment passed, giving women the right to vote. This is a great day for women, but not the best day to be born *if* you're a woman. June 4th natives of the female variety have a very hard time settling on long-term love. They fall in love quickly, but then find themselves bored. Then they either end the relationship completely or stray, and the cycle will repeat itself over and over again. June 4th men have some of the same romantic problems, though they can be less obsessed with creating a family and sometimes choose to remain bachelors. Women born on this day often go into childrearing with the bitter intention of raising their own children exactly opposite to how they themselves were raised.

⚡ JUNE 5

The world is your oyster, June 5th-er. You just walk through life, plucking the sweet, fat fruit from the trees that submissively bend their bows to you. Even when bad things happen, you truly believe that the Universe will find a way to right the wrongs. Also, people really like you. That sunny spirit just attracts friends left and right. It's highly likely that everyone secretly resents you, but, hey, if that's the worst of your problems, you're in pretty good shape.

⚡ JUNE 6

The happiest day of a June 6th native's life is his or her wedding day. Not for the usual reasons of marrying the love of their life, *et cetera*, but for the very practical reason that they no longer have to deal with their own finances. Their spouse may not know this yet, but eventually the June 6th-er will completely abdicate the bookkeeping and hand over all control. Hopefully the day will never come when two people born on June 6th tie the knot. Those two are in big trouble.

⚡ JUNE 7

Who's the best? If you were born on June 7, your answer was an immediate and excited, *"I am!"* You think an awful lot of yourself, and position yourself to be the favorite child, the teacher's pet, the office suck-up, and the community do-gooder, just to continually prove to others (and yourself) how great you are. While this is all slightly pathetic, your dedication to being the most awesome possible version of yourself is fairly impressive.

⚡ JUNE 8

What did the *Ghostbusters* do when they weren't able to find work as professors in the field of paranormal studies? Did they lie down and quit? Did they just give up on their dreams? NO. They banded together to start their own business, ridding the city of pesky urban ghosts—and ended up *saving* New York City. June 8th natives show the same tenacity as the *Ghostbusters*, never giving up in the face of disappointments or green slime. If one door is closed, they'll find a window, even if that means they have to climb up to the third story. They will get beat down over and over again, and always come back for more, for better or worse. Fun fact for fact fans: *Ghostbusters* was released on June 8, 1984.

⚡ JUNE 9

The middle of the night seems different when you're all alone, right, June 9th-er? You know what it's like to toss and turn and not be able to sleep. You know how relieved the streetlights seem to feel when they flicker off as the first light of dawn hits the pavement. If you were born on this day and currently sleep well, enjoy it. It won't last and soon enough you'll find yourself up, usually waking at the same time each night, flipping between late night telemercials and soft porn on cable.

⚡ JUNE 10

June 10th natives will give a shockingly different interpretation of their life each time you see them. Sometimes life is incredible, lucky, brilliant, and they're on a rocket aimed straight for the stars. Other times they're destitute, terrified, and a total failure. While the Gemini Twins usually speak out of both sides of the mouth, people born on this date are particularly dramatic in their desperately polarized, positive and negative narratives.

⚡ JUNE 11

Does your stomach hurt when you're stressed out, June 11th-er? Do you get a headache right at your temples when you're disappointed? People born on this day usually construct a whole physical-mental-emotional cause-and-effect that requires a great deal of explanation to health care professionals. Says your doctor, "Hmm, I've never seen a case where an itchy toe came from feeling under-appreciated at work. Let's go ahead and prescribe some anti-anxiety meds." Note: anti-anxiety meds will most probably clear up all your ailments.

⚡ JUNE 12

The devil is in the details. June 12th natives will find themselves thwarted by their lack of detail-orientation again and again. They have big-picture goals, and high ambitions for both their professional and family lives, but their failure to plan adequately regularly prevents their intentions from becoming realities. For example, if they're planning a birthday party, they'll get all the details right but forget to mail the invitations, or if they're applying for a new job, they'll get their interview time wrong.

⚡ JUNE 13

The cutting edge is the place where June 13th natives feel comfortable. They'll do everything in their power to make sure their image is hardcore and they are seen as untamable. This usually equates to risk-taking behaviors. Many celebs with major issues share this birthday, including tabloid favorites Mary-Kate and Ashley Olsen, ex-con Tim Allen, Siegfried of the ill-fated duo Siegfried and Roy, and the world-famous dumbass Steve-O from the absurd daredevil show *Jackass*.

⚡ JUNE 14

If you were born on June 14, look around at your colleagues the next time you have a meeting. Do you notice the squinted eyes glaring at you from around the room? See the turned-down mouths and hear the clipped tone in the voices of those around you? Yeah, that's because you kind of suck to work with. You're smart, but you spout all these ideas riddled with buzz words that sound good to upper management, and then you expect the rest of the team to implement those ideas. This makes you a frustrating manager and torturous peer, but you will probably keep getting promoted because your boss's boss thinks you actually do something well.

⚡ JUNE 15

People born on June 15 have something to say. They have *a lot* to say, actually, and if you're not on board with their point of view, they will launch a full-on, to-the-death battle against you. They are, however, far too polite, social, and fun-loving to ever actually let their opponent know about the fight. Their attention span is usually too short for them to act on their anger, so they won't even hold a grudge after their imaginary fight is over.

⚡ JUNE 16

There is nothing more frustrating than trying to make plans with someone born on June 16. These people are anxious to please, so they're like, "Well, where do *you* want to go?" And then, when given an answer, they launch into a lengthy conversation weighing the pros and cons of the suggested location. This conversation will be circuitous and unproductive, and will eventually lead to a totally different plan, which will once again be picked apart in another one-sided debate. The plans will eventually diffuse into something like, "Let's just play it by ear." The good thing about June 16th natives is that when they do come up with spontaneous plans, they usually channel their creativity into suggesting something really *kickass*.

⚡ JUNE 17
A June 17th native has major trust issues. They are extremely wary of trusting their hearts to others, and end up fabricating tons of obstacles to potential love affairs in an effort to not get hurt. M.C. Escher was born on June 17, and it's easy to see that his drawings are representative of the effort that others would have to go to in order to win the love of a June 17th-er.

⚡ JUNE 18
A super-fun activity to do with someone born on June 18 is to secretly record your conversations. They literally have *no* idea how they sound when they speak. No matter how many times that people born on this date hear that they're abrasive, rude, and bossy, they simply don't see it that way. They see themselves as being real, honest, and assertive, but if they ever actually heard themselves in conversation, chances are they'd be horrified—just like everyone else is!

⚡ JUNE 19
People born on June 19 are attention whores, plain and simple. They're like that because they were beautiful, precocious children and all the adults positively rewarded them for their charming qualities. They only want to hang out with people who fawn all over them, and definitely only want to date people who

lavish them with attention and gifts. These people are likely to break out into song and dance if the conversation slows down for a moment, and attempt wild stunts to ensure everyone's eyes are on them.

⚡ JUNE 20

Some people like to push themselves outside of their comfort zone to achieve goals or grow emotionally. Not June 20th natives. They have a very distinct comfort zone and hate to venture outside of it for any reason. It takes a great deal of outside help to get them to change unhealthy habits, and even when people born on this day attempt to make a change, it just doesn't seem to stick. They have modest goals and primarily just want to be left in peace as they go through the motions of their base little life.

⚡ GEMINI–CANCER CUSP

People born between June 19 and June 23 are on the cusp of Gemini and Cancer. These people may avoid situations that make them *feel* in order to maintain their composure. When they do experience their feelings fully, they tend to cry and laugh hysterically, attracting the attention of everyone around them. It's pretty embarrassing, so they usually refuse to go to sad movies, funerals, stand-up comedy shows, and any events taking place in the rural south.

CONTEMPTIBLE CANCER

JUNE 22 TO JULY 22

You have sooooo many feelings, Cancer, and that's exactly why you're so very contemptible. Other signs of the zodiac can keep it together and play it cool while you're just weeping all over the place. Tears of joy, tears of sorrow, tears of confusion... you cry them all. You get sniffly when you meet a kindred spirit, or when you fall short of a professional goal, or when you see a commercial for an Apple product. Everything just feels so dreadfully deep and serious and soggy when you're around.

Look, your cosmic symbol is the *crab*. (*Side note*: Don't get all excited about the sixty-nine-shaped astrological symbol. It certainly does not mean you're some superstar lover, though it does mean that you like to give as much—or more—than you like to receive.) Anyway, you would do well to take a lesson from the crab and develop a hard outer shell. Then, people would have some barrier between themselves and your feelings.

Cancer, be honest, are you at your healthiest right now? If you can't see your toes, or you wheeze when you're walking to the mailbox, you might want to take a general assessment of your habits. Are you exercising enough? Are you living a healthy lifestyle? Or are you eating full cans of frosting with a spoon and washing it down with a Big Gulp? You could blame the obesity gene, but Cancers are prone to calming their nervous emotions with Twinkies or other tasty junk foods.

Remember that novel called *The Shining*? OK, well, do you at least remember the movie? Well, Cancers often have a little bit of "the shining," with strong intuition and a connection with their past lives. They are really sensitive to their surroundings, and if one part of a Cancer's life is in disorder, it can ripple through to every other aspect. They use their psychic tendencies to justify wearing questionable clothing such as tie-dye T-shirts featuring a wolf howling at the moon, or long velour dresses with tattered hems, or anything with black lace and a fringe. Cancers are not known for their fashion-forward choices.

LOVE AND RELATIONSHIPS WITH CONTEMPTIBLE CANCER

Cancers throw their love around like a 50-lb kettlebell. They hurl it at whoever's closest and are shocked when it knocks out their love interest. They need to share their feelings about *everything*, from the weather to work to the unknown future. Cancers also can be emotionally needy and require constant affirmations about their partner's feelings.

If you are a Cancer, you probably know the name of the person you woke up next to. That's because you are not very good at promiscuity, even though the idea of it makes you happy. If for some reason you do *not* know the name of the other sweaty body wrapped up in the sheets, you will find it out soon enough through online stalking and other fact-checking methods. Then you will promptly scare off that person by professing your undying love for him or her on the second date. There are three rules you should follow to advance your relationships to the next level. Number one, strike the word "love" from your vocabulary until the other person says it. Numero deux, only one text or 'phone call *per day* should originate from you for the first year of courtship. And thirdly, don't talk about your feelings for more than two minutes at a time. Set a timer on your smartphone if you have to. If you *do* know the name of the person you woke up next to, your long-term relationship would probably benefit from following the above rules as well.

Cancers make good spouses for the longer term, if you can tolerate the endless flow of emoting. They do have a tendency to get jealous and suspicious, and their unfounded accusations can often rock the love boat. They take very good care of their families, constantly checking in to make sure everyone's feeling okay, but they don't take particularly good care of themselves. If you're dating a fit Cancer now, enjoy it while you can—because chances are that, as they age, they will get very fat. It's a good idea to create family traditions surrounding exercise and nutritious eating. While your family will certainly look ridiculous in your matching bike shorts or dance troop T-shirts, the tradition will keep the Cancerian committed to keeping fit and staying healthy.

CHECKLIST FOR DATING A CONTEMPTIBLE CANCER

You'll need at least half of these things in order to have a successful relationship with a Cancer.

Issues: Cancers love helping others work through their issues. They love nothing more than a fixer-upper friend or lover. So, if you have issues, don't hesitate to put them all out on the table for a Cancer to solve.

Thick skin: Don't get caught up in Cancer's drama. Be the bigger person and avoid being bogged down by their daily turmoil.

Good taste in food and drink: Cancers really love to get their grub on, so skip the drive thru and find something unique and interesting to wow them at the dinner table.

Tact: Cancerian feelings can get so easily hurt that—if you're not tactful when you communicate—you could damage the relationship. You can ask, "What time does the movie start?" and they'll hear, "I can't believe you're not ready yet. You suck."

Health insurance: Getting serious with a Cancer might mean that you often end up at the doctor's office. If you don't have good insurance, all those check-ups, therapy sessions, and prescriptions could add up.

Honesty: Cancers can tell usually when you're lying to them. If you're considering hitting and quitting, a Cancer will sniff you out a mile away.

CONTEMPTIBLE CANCER COMPATIBILITY

CANCER AND ARIES LOVE

In this match, the Ram runs the show and keeps the Crab on an emotional leash, pulling back on the choke chain whenever they feel like it. Cancer prefers to stay home and bake a pie, while Aries is happy going out to make their living in the world and meeting people. Aries does like pie, though, so if they can keep it together long enough to get to dessert, this match could be tolerable.

CANCER AND TAURUS LOVE

These two can get along well until Taurus puts his or her foot down about watching the football game instead of *Dancing with the Stars*, and Cancer will begin to sulk and employ the always-effective silent treatment. The odds of getting an apology from a Taurus—one that's acceptable to a Cancer—is so slim that the silent treatment could last for weeks. It's like siege warfare. But if you secretly enjoy the occasional multiday, passive-aggressive battle... this romance could be for you.

CANCER AND GEMINI LOVE

This match is a little like the fable of young Gemini-locks stumbling into the home of the Three Crabs.

The Gemini is tempted by the comfortable chair, the warm porridge, and the soft, soft pillow of the Cancer. If Gemini-locks finds the Cancer who is "just right," he or she may never leave.

CANCER AND CANCER LOVE

There's a sliding scale of acceptable sappiness in a relationship, depending on what's going on in the world and with the couple themselves. Two Cancers together will almost always surpass this reasonable level of romantic, sentimental syrup, thus alienating all their friends—those either in or out of couples. This will ultimately lead to the Cancers spending every single Saturday night indoors, lovingly supporting one another's movie suggestions while holding hands and eating junk food—and wearing matching Snuggies on the couch. "Sounds incredible," both Cancers say... at exactly the same time.

CANCER AND LEO LOVE

Leo likes having his or her ego stroked, and Cancer is a very good stroker. It's fairly inequitable for the Cancer, but as long as the Leo makes a minimal effort to placate the Cancer's tumultuous feelings, the relationship could last as long as weeks.

CANCER AND VIRGO LOVE

The main issue in a Cancer-Virgo match is that the Cancer can be a lazy ass while the Virgo is a real worker bee. Also, Virgo thinks he or she is much smarter, which may or may not be the case. If those issues are resolved, then the only remaining problem is that this couple will go from very little physical lovin' to almost none over the course of a few years. Add kids and careers to the picture, plus soccer games and in-laws, and this couple may as well embrace the idea of separate bedrooms.

CANCER AND LIBRA LOVE

Having nice things is important to this couple. They want to surround themselves with beauty and elegance, even if this means their credit card bills are *ugly*. Unless one of them is an heiress or Internet tycoon, the household finances could definitely be a problem.

CANCER AND SCORPIO LOVE

Watching a Cancer-Scorpio couple fight is like watching toddlers argue over who gets to play with a toy. One will take the toy, the other will cry, the other will take it back... then maybe there's some light kicking action... then someone gets distracted and bored with the fight, and before you know it they're playing nicely in the sandbox again.

CANCER AND SAGITTARIUS LOVE

Cancer wants to marry Sagittarius from the moment they first exchange smooches. Sagittarius might need ten years of convincing. This leads to problems and many fights that include choice phrases from Cancer such as, "Why don't you looooove me?" and, "What do I have to do to get you to commit to me?" Sagittarius responds with something like, "Baby, I just want to take my time and enjoy this. Let's not rush it," and, "It's not about a ring on your finger.

We're so much more than that," and, "What do you mean you went through my cell 'phone and text-told every person of the opposite sex to stay away from me?!"

CANCER AND CAPRICORN LOVE

If Capricorn would stop working for five minutes and take Cancer out on a date once in a while, the Capricorn would be richly rewarded. Though Cancers aren't great at dealing with their own stress, they are helpful at helping Capricorn to talk through their issues at work and their many plans for the future.

CANCER AND AQUARIUS LOVE

Check please! Because Cancer wants to go home and get to bed by nine p.m., as usual. All Aquarius's friends are here, everyone's having a good time, and Cancer suddenly doesn't feel good. Aquarius knows that putting Cancer in a taxi and sending him or her home alone will only lead to weeks of the silent treatment. Eh, the silent treatment isn't *that* bad. Bye, Cancer! Another round if you please, bartender, my good man...

CANCER AND PISCES LOVE

Hello? Is anyone in there? Cancer may feel like their Pisces other is never really present. Pisces, on the other hand, will feel like the Cancer is always ever-present—or even over-present—with seemingly unending queries about feelings, plans, ideas, and intuitions. This match is a tricky one and should be avoided for sanity's sake.

CAREER AND MONEY FOR CONTEMPTIBLE CANCER

Cancers are the type of coworkers who bake cookies and bring them into the office, leaving them strategically in a well-trafficked public space. They are the people who lean on your office or cubicle door and ask how your weekend was, how your kids are, how your dog is, and how your mother-in-law's parakeet is feeling. They actually care about you, which makes them terrible colleagues, because maybe if they'd leave you alone to get some work done, you could actually leave the office and go hang out with your real friends. Cancers also tend to have health issues—allergies, sensitivities, conditions—and so they really complicate group functions with demands for gluten-free, soy-free, nut-free, fun-free vegan cakes for the office celebrations.

Cancers actually make decent bosses, though. They're not too demanding and are ultimately approachable if an employee has a legitimate personal problem. Unfortunately, the Cancerian intuition lets them see through lame excuses and if you try to pull the wool over their eyes, you're setting yourself up for a long talk about their feelings. Cancerian bosses will also probably implement a lot of workplace programs, and hang posters with inspirational messages all over the hallways. Hang in there!

As Cancer workers build their careers, they make decisions based on intuition. They like to climb the ladder, but want to make sure they don't trade their emotional well-being for money. They just need to feel like they're doing something good for the world. Lots of Cancers end up in the healthcare profession and in politics, though they can be prone to depression when they reflect on how totally and completely screwed-up both systems actually are.

Cancers have a tendency to make and save their money. A Cancer is a good person to hit up to "borrow" some money because a) they probably have it; and b) they just want everyone to be happy, so they'll gladly cough it up.

ABSOLUTE WORST JOBS FOR A CONTEMPTIBLE CANCER

Corporate tax attorney: Look, a corporate tax attorney would be a miserable job for anyone, but for a Cancer it's totally unbearable. It's the perfect storm of endless paper pushing, the cold and heartless implementation of rules, long hours away from home, and a dress code that doesn't allow for stretch pants and house dresses.

Restructuring consultant: A Cancer should not be the person who decides who to hire and who to fire during a corporate restructure. While they can try to make decisions based only on performance statistics, they are likely to overlook or explain away the poor performance of someone who is a kind person.

Handyman: Cancers have a vision of what they want to accomplish when they take on a manual task, but because they can get distracted and trust their intuition (rather than a measuring tape), the final product isn't always exactly Pinterest-worthy.

JOBS THAT A CONTEMPTIBLE CANCER MIGHT NOT SCREW UP

Pet psychic: Cancers are not only incredibly intuitive, they are also animal lovers. They feel a deep connection with both people and pets, and can help you understand a little more about your pup's deep-seeded resentment toward squirrels, and how your cat's past lives are affecting her appetite.

Hospice nurse: If anyone's going to help make you comfortable as you shuffle loose this mortal coil, it should be a Cancer. They will go out of their way to help you ease your pain, like picking up chocolates for you from the corner store, arranging your flowers by the window so you can see them, and slipping you some extra morphine when they can.

High school history teacher: Nobody likes a teenager. They're surly, they don't listen, they plug themselves into terrible music, and usually have poor hygiene. But Cancers have a knack for communication. They can cut through the noise and actually transmit the signal. They appreciate history and revere old relics and traditions.

STARS OF THE SIGN CONTEMPTIBLE CANCER

The thing about Contemptible Cancers is that they're not a particularly flashy bunch. They are emotionally intense and enjoy staying in and around the home. This isn't a perfect recipe for fame and fortune. Look for that mom who's hugging her child tight after he's scraped his knee—she's probably a Cancer. The young man reading on the park bench instead of working for a living—quite possibly another Cancer. The obese woman in a tie-dye T-shirt with a unicorn and the full Moon, walking a ferret on a leash. She is absolutely, *definitely* a Cancerian.

There are a few celebrity Cancers who exemplify the most contemptible aspects of the sign. Tom Cruise, for example, has demonstrated his ability to portray people with very intense feelings. His passion for Scientology also really shows the philosophical, spiritual side of a Cancer. And his super-weird behavior shows how frail the Cancer's rationality can be in the face of emotions.

Cancers appreciate good food and drink, so it's no wonder that many world-famous chefs fall under the sign of the Crab. Anthony Bourdain, Wolfgang Puck, and Jamie Deen are all Cancers. Some Cancers have been able to channel their excess emotions onto paper to become famous writers. Classic authors Henry David Thoreau, Franz Kafka, Nathaniel Hawthorne, and George Orwell are all Cancers. Some Cancers who weren't able to properly channel their intuitive spirit into positive endeavors turned criminal. Those include depression-era mobsters Machine Gun Kelly and John Dillinger, and—of course—the craziest Cancerian of them all... Lizzie Borden (who took an ax and gave her mother forty whacks).

CONTEMPTIBLE CANCER BIRTHDAYS

⚡ GEMINI–CANCER CUSP

If you were born between June 19 and June 23, your birthday falls into the Gemini-Cancer Cusp. This means that you embody aspects of both the Twins of Gemini and the Crab of Cancer. You are spontaneous and emotional, which makes you a difficult date for a movie or play. You guffaw loudly when something's funny and sob big tears when something's sad. It's a spectacle and—though it's obvious you can't help it—it just seems a little tacky.

⚡ JUNE 21

You're just a fool in love, aren't you, Cancer? In fact... the pursuit of love has likely made a fool of you several times. The bad news is that you'll likely continue to make a fool of yourself into your old age. The good news is you don't care what the haters say about YOU or the people you foolishly adore. "We do not judge the people we love," as Jean-Paul Sartre (a June 21st-er, philosopher, and infamous misogynist) famously said.

⚡ JUNE 22

"This is NOT about me." If you were born on June 22, practice saying this over and over and over, and then you can go out in public again and be with your friends—if they'll still have you. Stop butting in to other people's conversations and hijacking their emotions. Others are allowed to quibble, converse, ponder, and stress without it turning you to a big pile of sticky, sad rubble.

JUNE 23

"Wait till they get a load of me." Tim Burton's *Batman* was "born" (released) on June 23 in 1989, and—like its star character, The Joker—you consider yourself quite the comedian. Others may or may not agree. Also, like The Joker, you probably have an arch-nemesis that you keep crossing paths with. It's unlikely that person knows that you exist, meaning the rivalry is all in your head. Don't be crazy or turn to a life of random, sadistic crime.

JUNE 24

There are 24 hours in a day, and if you were born on June 24, chances are that you're drinking or eating (or thinking about drinking or eating) during most of those hours. You self-medicate with too much food and alcohol. Truth be told, it's probably better to grab another chocolate bar than to damp down all your feelings, though... you don't want to turn out like mass murderer Charles Whitman, who was born on this day.

JUNE 25

Is it 2nd Street and 4th Avenue, or 4th Street and 2nd Avenue? Are you bringing twelve chickens at two o'clock, or two chickens at twelve o'clock. You have NO idea, do you, Cancer? People born on this date are notoriously inexact in their communication and their comprehension of the world. You just don't really think that the small details matter. Sorry to say, they DO matter. A notebook would probably help you quite a lot.

JUNE 26

If you were born on June 26 and have children, you are probably one of "those" parents who want to make sure your children have all the comforts—both emotional and material—that money can buy. If you don't have kids yet, you probably swear you'll never be one of "those" parents... But just you wait.

⚡ JUNE 27

Other people's kids are terrible, right? At least that's how you see the snotty little brats that your friends parade around, as though dropping a deuce in the potty was on a par with abolishing world hunger. The truth is, your kids will be terrible too, so if you've been considering sterilization, you might want to go ahead with that.

⚡ JUNE 28

What keeps you up at night? If you were born on this day, people have been telling you to "get over it" for years... but whatever IT is... it's not so easy for you to shake. Go see a psychiatrist—one that prescribes the good meds—and that should help you forget.

⚡ JUNE 29

Some people born on June 29 are so idealistic that they become incredibly obnoxious. They won't eat at such-and-such restaurant because it uses non-recyclable napkins, and they won't speak to the neighbors because they purchased their dog at a pet store instead of rescuing it. When called out on how difficult they make real life for everyone else, they cry. These people are not fun to have as children, and even as adults you might spot them wailing on the floor in a department store about the injustices of commercial fishing.

⚡ JUNE 30

You are a bottomless pit, June 30th native. You can't really seem to get "full" when you eat, and can't get enough of your lovers, your family, your kids, money, and so on and so forth. Because of this, you are either constantly consuming or you feel empty. Them's the breaks.

⚡ JULY 1

If you were born on July 1, you can probably track your moods by your "recent calls" list. Go ahead, take a look! You have certain people you call when you're feeling blue, others you call when you're feeling oppressed and put-upon, and most of your cell 'phone plan's monthly minutes are spent on a small group who you call when you're feeling ultra-murderous.

⚡ JULY 2

Some scientists argue that the number of things an average person can keep in their working memory is 7 (plus or minus 2)... Referred to as Miller's Law, this is why phone numbers have 7 numbers. If you, July 2nd Cancer, are a "7 minus 2"—as in, not the sharpest crayon in the box—you tend to beat yourself up about it, wondering why you're not as clever as everyone else. If you're a "plus 2," you may be too busy worrying about what everyone else is thinking about to take advantage of the extra brain space.

⚡ JULY 3

Because they often have a disorganized lifestyle, July 3rd natives may not be careful about their health and nutritional habits. When they are young this isn't a problem, but as they approach middle age this habit can become dangerous, especially if they don't exercise regularly.

⚡ JULY 4

How hard is it to get an apology out of someone born on July 4? You'd better gather evidence worthy of a federal case if you want to convince someone born on this day that they've done anything wrong. You're much more likely to get a combination of righteous indignation, passive-aggressive annoyance, endless argument, and finger-pointing than an outright apology. If they DO apologize, you'd better look deeper, because they've probably done something else wrong that you don't even know about yet!

⚡ JULY 5

Where's that to-do list, July 5th native? Is it there, under all the unread novels? Or over there, by the chair that you bought at a garage sale and started refinishing? Is it by the beginner's knitting kit? Or there by the half-finished puzzle? Your goals far exceed your attention span.

⚡ JULY 6

Some great people share this birthday, such as the current Dalai Lama, who is an activist as well as a political and spiritual leader, and Frida Kahlo, the inspired Mexican painter. Also a July 6th native is perhaps the most brilliant philosopher and most gifted painter of all time... recent American president George W. Bush. People born on this day want to share their natural-born gifts with the world. Sometimes it's cool; sometimes it's not.

⚡ JULY 7

Almost all your energy is spent trying to rectify your vision of life with actual, real existence. If this is your birthday, you might have a job in marketing or public relations, you describe your friendships and relationships as much more fulfilling than they actually are, and you often visit the doctor to discuss ailments that are usually non-existent. Make your fantasy life a little more interesting!

⚡ JULY 8

You've got 99 problems, but your spouse ain't one of them... if you're married or otherwise hitched, you might think of your spouse as you would think of a particularly comfortable piece of furniture. If you're not in a long-term relationship, commitment is low on your priority list. Work and play seem much more important than falling into a mundane, daily routine with someone who's only going to get fatter and less happy than they currently are.

⚡ JULY 9

If you're close to a July 9th native, you can think of them as an onion. They reveal very little about their real feelings, their past, and their goals—and until you find a way to break down their walls, you'll never know what they really want or expect out of life. Also, they might actually stink of onions, because they're likely to be taking a bunch of weird health supplements.

⚡ JULY 10

July 10th-ers are freaking needy. They want lots of praise about their excellent work ethic and want you to admire all their unique things, and all the gifts they give to others, and they want to know how you feel about them, and how you see your relationship evolving, and what you want to eat for dinner, and how you liked every single bite of every single dish. Better to avoid people born on this date unless you have a LOT of time on your hands.

⚡ JULY 11

On July 11, 1960, Harper Lee published *To Kill a Mockingbird*, featuring the engimatic character "Boo" Radley. Boo was kind of a recluse—quiet, slightly creepy—but eventually he proved to be a good guy. That's a pretty good analogy for your personality, if you were born on July 11. It's not that you don't like people; it's just that you hate being around them.

⚡ JULY 12

There's being close to your family, and there's being TOO close to your family, and if you were born on July 12, you skate that thin line. Dial it back by fifty per cent and it's probably an appropriate amount of togetherness for preserving sanity. You've probably gone on one or two (maybe more) "epic trips" in your life and constantly reference your cathartic experiences in that foreign culture, whether it was Kansas or Korea.

⚡ JULY 13

Just because you're dating someone who's served time, drinks too much, talks down to you, and doesn't like your family, it doesn't mean that you have terrible, terrible taste in the opposite sex. (Note: if you're reading this and happen to be dating someone without those characteristics, you can just replace the above list with their own negative qualities). All it "means" is that you are slightly twisted and choose to make everything— even your love life—both a learning experience and an adventure. It also probably means that you're too scared to change your life, even when your life sucks.

⚡ JULY 14

July 14 is the date that Jane Goodall arrived in the African jungle to study chimps in their natural habitat. If this is your birthday, you may also find yourself surrounded by monkeys, or at least that's how it feels sometimes. Luckily you have a quick, witty tongue and can hold your own against the natives, though you may find yourself very annoyed with the whole thing.

⚡ JULY 15

Plop-plop-fizz-fizzzz!! If you were born on this day, you are probably quite familiar with Alka Seltzer, Tums, Rolaids, Gas-X, ginger-ale, and all other medicinal and homeopathic treatments recommended for treating overindulgence. You just can't help yourself from overdoing it with food and booze, and often find yourself in a spiral of plucking the hair of the dog that bit you.

⚡ JULY 16

Who IS that mystery lady (or gentleman)? If you were born on July 16, you love to weave a sense of mystery around yourself and really love to get other people murmuring and speculating about what you're up to. It's just nice to not be alone in wondering what the hell you're doing with your life, right?

JULY 17

"Come into my parlor," said the spider to the fly..."
If you are a July 17th native, you are the fly in this
scenario. And, unfortunately, you are doomed to
succumb to the flattering spider over and over again.
You just don't have the capacity to wise up and stop
getting caught up in the web. Sorry about that.

JULY 18

People born on July 18 have NO business having all
that extra money... they don't work very hard, they can't
hold down a job, and most of the time they're not into
nefarious dealings—yet, somehow, they always get by
and have a little extra in their pocket. Something truly
cosmic butters their bread.

JULY 19

It's not a performance problem, it's an expectations
problem... or maybe it's a perspective problem. July
19th natives just want toooo much. They want to be
able to tell people their innermost secrets—the real
"freak flag" stuff—and not scare potential friends and
lovers away. That is not an easy feat in today's cynical
world, so people born on this day might go through life
feeling generally unsatisifed with the depth of their
relationships.

JULY 20

Do you ever feel like you're living in a fairy tale?
Like life is just sooo good that you just find yourself
humming show tunes while you mop the kitchen floor
or while you sexually service your significant other? If
you were born on July 20, you probably live in a strange,
blissful little world that sometimes camouflages the

terrible things that are happening right under your nose. In fact, it is more likely than not that people born on this day are dating, or married to, *total creeps* but just haven't woken up to the fact yet.

⚡ JULY 21

Sometimes, people born on July 21 experience major problems because of their desire to be unique and interesting. Robin Williams and Ernest Hemingway both felt this pressure and turned to alcohol, and many natives of this day do try to spice up their lives with some sort of substance abuse. The pang doesn't go away, though, when you look in the mirror and realize that you are a hack with average talent.

⚡ JULY 22

Natives of this day are so argumentative that it's hard for friends and family to be around them. Usually, others just grit their teeth and endure a social engagement with a July 22nd-er, wait for him or her to leave, and then talk about the terrible bore behind its back. Nobody wants to hurt your feelings, of course. If this is your birthday, the only way to stop others from dissing you is to simply never leave the room. Ever.

⚡ CANCER–LEO CUSP

People born between July 19 and July 23 embody characteristics of both Cancers and Leos. You have more energy and present yourself better than most Cancers do, with an attention to your physical appearance and a focus on your career. Unlike most Leos, you care about other people as much or more than yourself, which makes you a pretty cool pal to have around.

LAME LEO
JULY 23 TO AUGUST 22

I f you're a Leo, the odds are very good you've flipped to this page and these are the first words you're reading in *Bad Birthdays*. Welcome, Lame Leo. As you probably already know, dear Leo, your kind can be self-focused and egocentric. You don't put a lot of energy into understanding other peoples' perspectives... unless, that is, you think being empathetic will eventually result in extra attention for you.

When Leos interact with others, they make a big show of it. They can be embarrassingly over-the-top with romantic gestures and gift giving, and if their efforts are not duly praised, they sulk. If a cousin you barely know just sent you a pet robot—or a similarly absurd and showy holiday gift—he or she is likely to be a Leo. If a female co-worker just received two-dozen roses delivered to work, or a singing telegram, chances are she is dating a Leo—and has yet to sleep with him. Once the chase is over, the charismatic Lion tends to lose interest in its prey. (Get the poor gal a box of tissues, she'll need it.) They are loyal when they finally settle down, but for many Leos that may occur only after years of sowing their wild oats.

Leos are drawn to public speaking and performance arts, always making sure that they're noticed and appreciated. They are often funny and have a great sense of timing, always delivering their lines to have maximum impact. Hollywood and Broadway are both full of Leos, and an alphabetical list of famous Leos would take up much more space and time than we have here in this book.

The natural charisma that Leos possess draws people to them, and when a Leo feels a connection with another person, it's pretty hard to shake them off. If you're thinking about befriending a Leo, be aware that it's basically a lifelong commitment. Even when you're in the retirement home, Leo will be sitting next to you, telling dirty jokes and making the staff chuckle. They are loyal friends, and when they put down their metaphorical cane and top hat, and slip off their fictional tap shoes, they can be genuinely kind and warm.

LOVE AND RELATIONSHIPS WITH LAME LEO

If a Leo locks you in his or her romantic sights, sorry to say you are probably a goner. They are dedicated to the hunt and will stop at nothing to conquer you. The bad news is that, once they do, they might find themselves wandering around and noticing other people they'd like to conquer. The good news is that they have a reputation for being terrific in bed, so at least it will be fun.

It often takes Leos a long time to find their soul mate and settle down with one partner, and they'll play the field for as long as they can, keeping all their options open. Once they throw in the towel and settle for one person, their loyalty surfaces and they can become possessive, territorial, and a bit obsessive. They want to fulfill the roles of lover, mother, father, best friend, and spoiled child—all rolled into one—and they always feel like they're the ones in the relationship who are the most in love. Again, this is annoying, but usually worth it because of their natural prowess between the sheets, grrr.

If you snuggle up with a Leo, know that they care a lot about appearance. Specifically, theirs. They preen before going out in public and choose their clothes carefully to be flattering and eye-catching. They are hungry for attention and will dress and accessorize to maximize impact. If you're romantically involved with a Leo, don't be too jealous or critical of the Leo's flashy ways, just focus on keeping them interested. Even though the Leo is a loyal friend, they may have loose standards when it comes to fidelity. They don't mean to stray, it's just that long-term relationships can get too boring for the big cat.

CHECKLIST FOR DATING A LAME LEO

You'll need at least half of these things in order to have a successful relationship with a Leo.

Assets: Ladies, show off that cleavage. Men, squeeze into some tight pants. You want to emphasize what you can bring to a Leo's boudoir.

Eagerness: Be ready to experiment and willing to try anything. Leos like to be spontaneous in romance. Quick! Spontaneity test: go to Google right now and type in "crotchless Spiderman outfit."

Compliments: Stroke their feline ego, praise their clothing, their choice of restaurant, their perfume, and so on.

Self-control: Remember the book *The Rules* that instructed women not to call men because men enjoy the hunt? Well, the rules totally apply to Leos of both genders. Let them pursue YOU. Don't act too clingy and try to keep the mystery alive as long as humanly possible.

A sense of humor: Laugh at a Leo's jokes, even if they're kind of lame, and try to enjoy them when they strut their stuff and show off.

Perspective: Leos can blow things out of proportion, both positively and negatively, and they can sulk for hours if they don't get their way. Just keep a sense of what's important so you can apologize and quickly end a fight by groveling, if need be.

LAME LEO COMPATIBILITY

LEO AND ARIES LOVE

Leo and Aries are both prideful and arrogant. Both are independent and strong-willed, and they can really make it work behind closed doors. But out in public, Leo might get self-conscious around Aries and their lack of social grace. The fights will be epic, but the good times could even it out.

LEO AND TAURUS LOVE

The problem with this match is that Leos and Tauri can both be too determined and too loyal for their own good. What should have been a one-night stand could be drawn out for weeks, months, and years just out of sheer stubbornness. You'd probably be better off not hooking up in the first place.

LEO AND GEMINI LOVE

This is a cute and playful love match, and watching the romance unfold is like watching kittens roll around and chase a ball of yarn together. Both signs have a tendency to wander, so there could be hurt feelings down the road, and Gemini will drive Leo a little batty with always wanting to rearrange the furniture depending on their mood swings.

LEO AND CANCER LOVE

Cancer just wants to be held. Leo just wants to be praised. If you can memorize these rules and not let your feelings get hurt every time someone forgets to spoon after making love, or fails to praise a new hairstyle, this romantic match could be tolerable. Leo will likely get bored with Cancer's neediness in the long run, which will cause serious ugly-crying from Cancer. It's a potential mess.

LEO AND **LEO** LOVE

In a relationship with two lions, there's bound to be a little biting and scratching. Whether it's the good kind or the bad kind is anyone's guess, and it could go either way. Leo's self-consciousness really surfaces when face-to-face with one of their own kind, so feelings could easily get hurt and egos bruised.

LEO AND **VIRGO** LOVE

Virgo thinks he or she is soooo smart, and is constantly psychoanalyzing all of Leo's shortcomings, and it stings a little bit. If they go out with friends, Virgo's always silently judging Leo's gregarious, charismatic nature. Leo might backlash and make fun of Virgo, and Virgo does not take that lightly. Get ready for a long, silent, angry car ride home... and you'd better make up the couch, because someone's going to be sleeping on it.

LEO AND **LIBRA** LOVE

If you find yourself in a Leo-Libra relationship, you should quickly memorize the phone numbers of the nearest florist, chocolatier, and 'adult items' shop, because you will both be spoiling each other with presents to keep the romance alive. Love is in the air, and the only thing that might dampen it is that the Libra may find themselves constantly making compromises in order to please Leo. Leo just takes and takes, and then takes a little bit more in this relationship.

LEO AND **SCORPIO** LOVE

A Leo-Scorpio combination is like a constant tug-of-war that neither side will give up. You're attracted to each other, you respect each other, but that doesn't mean either of you are just going to give up and let the other choose the restaurant. If you try to be stubborn *only* about things that actually matter, you'll only fight about half of the time.

LEO AND **SAGITTARIUS** LOVE

Leo, be warned... Sagittarius will actually *tell you* if you look fat in those jeans. The feline ego could take a licking if they enter this match, but the attraction is strong and Leo finds Sagittarius interesting and dynamic. It's definitely not the worst combination in the world, though it's unlikely that these two will be able to save up enough to end up on a yacht in their retirement years.

LEO AND **CAPRICORN** LOVE

Capricorn has one word for Leo. Tacky. Leos can be flashy in their clothes, accessories, and hairstyles, and Capricorn thinks it's all for the birds. Capricorns are boring old farts, anyway, Leo, so don't get your panties in a bunch about it.

LEO AND **AQUARIUS** LOVE

Leos are prideful people, and there are only a few signs that can bring them to their knees. Aquarius and Leo get along really well most of the time—both are social creatures, both enjoy being spontaneous and fun. But Leo will never feel like Aquarius gives him or her enough attention, enough credit, enough *love*. Leo could find themselves insecure and uncomfortable with Aquarius's indifferent approach to romantic relationships.

LEO AND PISCES LOVE

Leo and Pisces complement each other nicely, as long as Pisces doesn't mind a life of stroking Leo's ego and pumping up his or her self-confidence. For the most part, Pisces people usually don't seem to mind this kind of relationship imbalance, but if they DO mind... they'll make it clear with their constant moping and whining.

CAREER AND MONEY FOR LAME LEO

You can spot the office Leo from a mile away. He or she has a swagger, a sense of self-importance, and a considerably overblown opinion of their contribution to the workplace. They're also pretty good negotiators and usually aren't afraid to take risks, so chances are they're getting paid more than their colleagues. Female Leos still make the requisite average $.33 less than male Leos, though, in case you were thinking that the Lioness fared better than the female of other zodiac species. Anyway...

Leos are goal-oriented, and most of the time they are able to see past their enormous egos to take in the big picture. This allows them to strategize and plan for their eventual world domination—or at least their total military command of the office. They love to be in charge, and the higher up a Leo gets on the corporate ladder, the more their chest will swell with the pride of their accomplishments. Be warned, though. Leos are very, very charming, so in between all the amusing post-workhappyhours and prime-time-television-recap water-cooler chats, you might not notice how they're scheming to take your job until it's too late. They might not even mean to take your job, to be truthful. They're loyal friends and would never do a pal wrong on purpose. Most Leos are natural-born people persons, and so they might climb up in the ranks effortlessly. But doesn't that somehow make it even more obnoxious?

Young Leos in the workplace often find themselves frustrated. No one seems to notice how smart they are, how capable, and what a huge asset to the team they could be. They expect praise—and a lot of it—and when they don't receive their kudos they could end up shooting themselves in the foot by sulking and being generally uncooperative. If you are thinking about hiring a Leo as an intern or an assistant, you might want to consider getting a jar of stickers on your desk and handing them out when the Leo completes their tasks to satisfaction.

ABSOLUTE WORST JOBS FOR A LAME LEO

Undercover officer: On the surface, the job of an undercover officer or private investigator sounds like a glamorous career that would attract a Leo with an affinity for James Bond or film noir. These misguided Leos will quickly learn, however, that—in reality—

stakeouts and intelligence work is the kind of work Leos hate most. Most Lions would go crazy sitting for long hours on stakeouts or engaged in solo online research. Even if there's an occasional payoff—including kudos from their tight-lipped, mustachioed supervisor—the amount of unnoticed, detailed work that goes into a single case would conflict with a Leo's ego and desire to be in the spotlight.

Understudy or extra: This one's tricky, because Leos make terrific leading ladies or men on Broadway or in Hollywood, and sometimes it's necessary to work as an understudy or extra in order to earn the chance to lead the cast. However, seeing their name on a cast list as an understudy—just once too often—could drive a Leo to despair. They might sulk and start drinking heavily when they realize that their dreams are crumbling and they'll have to take their job as a waiter or escort a little more seriously.

Work-from-home customer service rep for big corporation: Leo hates the following: a) not playing by their own rules, b) people who are upset, and c) feeling isolated. So, while the expanding world and the concept of telecommuting are great for the more antisocial signs, a Leo would really hate going an entire day, week, month, etc., without personal interactions. Add irritated customers with mundane complaints and a Leo will start hyperventilating and sweating. Then, when they have to follow some corporate script instead of pursuing their own logic and intuition, they'll break out in literal or figurative hives and have to rush off to see the doctor.

JOBS THAT A LAME LEO MIGHT NOT SCREW UP

Jewelry maker: Leo knows how to use his or her hands. Not only do they like to purchase and collect fancy, shiny trinkets and baubles, they also have a natural ability to craft lovely accessories. Leos have a unique style, though their work might be on the flashy and gaudy side for the most tasteful collectors. But as long as there are little old ladies and trampy young gals with money to burn, a Leo will be able to make a good living in this field.

Politician: It's not that Leos are necessarily untruthful, it's more that they like to make people happy and they like being the center of attention. The Lions sometimes roar before they weigh out the ramifications of what they are saying. They can also promise different things to different people and not feel a pressing need to follow through. All of these characteristics make them perfect politicians. In fact, many politicians throughout history were born under the sign of the Leo, including Barack Obama, Bill Clinton, Herbert Hoover, Lyndon B. Johnson, and Bernito Mussolini.

Agent: Even though Leos are total hams and excel on the stage or in front of the camera, statistically not all of them will make it to the big-time. Becoming an agent can be a solid back-up career for a Leo, which will allow them to strut their stuff, give out lots of advice, and live vicariously through the success of their clients. Their pride will swell when they get their celebs a great gig, and they'll enjoy the peripheral excitement of a showbiz life with the perks of always having steady work.

STARS OF THE SIGN
LAME LEO

Leos are the stuff stars are made of. They glitter and glow and love being on stage and in the public eye. It's no wonder that some of history's most fabulous individuals are Leos. In fact, there are so many famous Leos that you can usually play connect-the-Leo in any showbiz project. For example, J.K. Rowling—author of the bestselling *Harry Potter* series—is a Leo, as are actors Daniel Radcliffe and Rupert Grint, who play Harry and Ronald in the movies. Similarly, Suzanne Collins—who wrote *The Hunger Games*—is a Lioness, as well as the star of the film adaptation, Jennifer Lawrence. Jennifer Lawrence stars in *X-Men: Days of Future Past* with Anna Paquin and Halle Berry, two other famous Lionesses.

The downside of Leos is that sometimes their desire to be the center of attention outweighs their sense of decorum and decency. Because of this unfortunate fact, there are too many reality television stars who embarrass themselves in front of millions of viewers each week, just to ensure they are in the limelight. *Real Housewife* Danielle Staub is a Leo, as are Spencer Pratt and Honey Boo Boo's mother—June Thompson.

LAME LEO BIRTHDAYS

⚡ CANCER–LEO CUSP

If your birthday falls between July 19 and July 23, you were born on the Cancer-Leo cusp. You should always carry tissues in your purse or glove compartment because you probably find yourself in tears fairly often. Sometimes you're a sad sack and are overcome with emotion, but at other times you find yourself just laughing and laughing until you cry. Try to get yourself under control—you're being watched. Literally. People are always watching you because you have an unique charisma that attracts a lot of attention.

⚡ JULY 23

If you were born on July 23, chances are you've already bloomed. People born on this day are destined to do something great. They usually do it early in life, then taper off to a more moderate success in their chosen field. Luckily, you'll be able to entertain your pals with stories for years to come about your one big break.

⚡ JULY 24

Where are you going? If you were born on this day, your constant changes in direction are making you dizzy. Slow down and don't give in to impulse, unless you enjoy giving your friends and family whiplash. It's possible that July 23rd-native Amelia Earhart—the famous, fearless pilot who disappeared over the Pacific in the 1930s—actually just changed her mind and flew over to Japan for some sushi, or to China for a peek at the Great Wall. Interestingly, July 24 is Pioneer Day in the state of Utah, which celebrates the polygamous Mormons who

123

flooded into the state to escape persecution in the late 1840s. So, there's another tactic for you to consider: if you can't make up your mind and decide on a single course of action, just choose all the wives.

⚡ JULY 25

Leos are known for their loyalty and pride-laden spirit. They're also known for their hot-n-sexy romantic streak. Unfortunately, this sometimes clashes, and people born on July 25 are especially prone to stray if they do decide to get married. The gorgeous and deadly Mata Hari, who was a spy during the First World War, was executed on July 25 and should live on as a symbol to all born on this day. Double-crossing will only end in despair.

⚡ JULY 26

If you were born on July 26, take a quick look through your Facebook friends. Oh my god, they're all losers, right? You are very clearly the most clever, successful, and interesting amongst your peer group. There's something about people born on this day that makes them flock to the less fortunate, which can be great if you run a charity, but terrible if you're looking for a date.

⚡ JULY 27

People born on July 27 hide their emotions from the world and try to maintain a stoic outlook on even the most tragic situations. Then, when they're alone, they shame-eat an entire pint of ice cream to help cover the pain. But then, so that no one knows about the binge, they go to the gym and run on a treadmill for two hours. All this effort just to seem in control. In other words, people born on this day should definitely find a good therapist.

⚡ JULY 28

July 28th-ers may often find themselves with their foot in their mouth after dealing out unintended insults. They respect and love their family and friends. However, they also have a strict ethical code and speak up when someone circumvents their personal rules. Others may see people born on this day as judgmental, prideful, and haughty... and they may find themselves left out of family reunions, office barbecues, and other social occasions.

⚡ JULY 29

Let's put on our nerd glasses and examine the number 729 for a moment. First of all, it's both a square and a cube. The number's also special because the first two integers add up to equal the last, and—hold on to your pocket protectors—the square root (27) and the cube root (9) are the same integers that make up the number, though in a different order (7-2-9... see?). So what does all this have to do with the lame attitude and behavior of people born on July 29? Like the number 729, natives of this day are versatile and work very hard. Unlike the numbers, they refuse to adhere to other people's standards and like to create their own rules, which makes them seem rebellious and cool when they're teenagers... but it gets old after a while.

⚡ JULY 30

Leos look after their families with ferocity for the most part, but people born on July 30 just can't stop living in the past. They remember all the little things done wrong to them in childhood—remember that time Mom didn't buy me ice cream after my recital, remember that time Dad blacked both of my eyes with a frying pan, etc.—and hold their parents at arm's length as adults as punishment for these past deeds. They try to find redemption in their own children, though they sometimes find that frustrating because children are terrible and rarely behave the way you want them to.

⚡JULY 31

If you were born on July 31, there's good news and bad news. The good news is that you're a natural persuader and could easily pursue a career as an attorney, publicist, or politician. The bad news is that, as you climb to the top, you leave a string of unhappy lovers behind you. Take heart, they're not unhappy because you didn't perform well. They just always wanted more than you were willing to give romantically. Once you do settle down, you might still find your love life in tumult, though your Leo loyalty will come out strongly (maybe too strongly) when you find the right partner.

⚡AUGUST 1

If you were born on this day, you are single-minded and ambitious. You set goals and accomplish them at all costs, even if it means neglecting the people who care about you the most. This is a lot like what MTV did to musicians on August 1, 1981, when it released the first music video of all time. MTV had a goal and a vision, and didn't mind trampling the status quo and hurting the feelings of less photogenic musicians in order to make that dream a reality. You can't even suppose that they didn't foresee the impact that videos would have on the music industry, considering the first song they released as a video was titled, *Video Killed the Radio Star*. Oh, they knew alright... and they went right ahead and carried on. Now the industry is filled with stars like

Miley Cyrus and songs like *Call Me Maybe* instead of music that really *means* something, Man. The point is, August-the-Firstian, just pay attention to the possible outcomes of your ambitions... because a single ripple can carry a long way and you can completely kill your dreams by turning them into reality. Get it?

AUGUST 2

If you were born on August 2, close your eyes and think back to the best moment of your life. In your heart of hearts, you probably feel—and are probably correct— that this epic moment was as good as it gets. The best times are behind you now, so just carry on and stay hopeful for the occasional Saturday-night lay, a good laugh with friends, or at least an exciting new television series that you can really look forward to. Life won't go downhill fast, it will just slowly—almost imperceptibly— decline until you die.

AUGUST 3

Sometimes haters are just gonna hate. But sometimes haters are actually right and your behavior stinks. For August 3rd natives, the challenge is to find the balance between these two positions. While people born on this day are unusually talented—and sometimes have trouble making friends because of others' jealousy— they also tend to defy the usual Leo loyalty and spread their affections far and wide. So, just hear the haters out and see if they're hating on *you* or on the way you behave, because maybe it actually IS all your fault.

AUGUST 4

Nobody's going to tell you how to live your life, right, August Fourthian? You are the rebel of the Leos, and are even more independent, prideful, and aggressive than others of your ilk. You have a big heart and are likely to be involved in charitable causes, which you think makes up for the fact that you treat the people in your life badly, but it doesn't. You're still kind of a jerk.

AUGUST 5

If this is your birthday, your inner Lion rears its head when someone disagrees with you openly. Nothing makes you more annoyed than someone who doesn't share the same opinion—because, let's face it, you *know what you're talking about.* If someone doesn't agree with you, it's clearly because they don't understand the issue, or they don't *really* care about it the way you care about it. You might be right, but that still doesn't make you a very good cocktail party guest.

AUGUST 6

Look around, August 6th native. Do you see lengthy to-do lists with only one or two items crossed off? Do you see piles of paperwork and bills that you're meaning to get to? How about the sink... is it full of dirty dishes? You just can't quite get it together, and here's why: *you are a lazy ass.* More specifically, your lazy habits disrupt your energy and ambition to get things done. So here comes a dose of tough love. Turn off the TV, put on some good tunes, and attack that to-do list one item at a time until you're king (or queen) of the jungle, as a Leo should be.

AUGUST 7

On August 7, 1974, daredevil Philippe Petit—also a Leo, don't-you-know?—illegally stretched a high wire between the twin towers of NYC's World Trade Center and walked it, becoming famous for the feat. This act represents two parts of an August-the-seventh-er's personality. First of all, people born on this day have the need to keep secrets, even if there's no reason to be secretive, just like Petit had to keep his kooky plans to himself. Secondly, these Leos love being in the spotlight, but have to get there in an unconventional way.

⚡AUGUST 8

Leos are known for their sense of humor and charismatic ways, but those born on August 8 break the mold a little bit. It's difficult to get them to laugh, and they worry about small things too much. If you're romantically involved with someone born on this day, help him or her loosen up and relax with some physical touch. August-the-Eighth-ers will purr if you pet them.

⚡AUGUST 9

People born on this day may not truly be vain, deep inside, but if it looks like a duck, and it walks like a duck... you see where this is headed. Whitney Houston was born on August 9, and she exemplifies the star power and charisma that these Leos can bring to the table, and also the fierce Leo loyalty with which they pursue even the most questionable of romantic partners.

⚡AUGUST 10

Your overriding characteristic is your constant indecision. Here are a few examples from your daily life:

You at the paint store: "I bought this gallon of Robin's Egg Blue, but after I painted half of my kitchen I realized I really wanted Seafoam Green. Can I switch it? Wait, what is that? English Lavender? That's the one I want. Oh, no, wait, the pink!"

You talking to a waiter: "I'm in the mood for chicken, I think. Wait, no, I had chicken for lunch. How about pasta. Ugh, pasta has too many carbs. Tuna? But is it full of mercury? Ok, ok, I'll have the Caprese salad."

You at the voting booth: "Uuuuh, I usually vote Democrat, but this guy's a real yahoo. Maybe I should vote Republican. But I'm for women's rights, and that guy's clearly not. But I don't care for the tax policy the female candidate supports. But... but... but..."

⚡AUGUST 11

Do you find yourself doing unhealthy things such as binge eating or drinking when you feel sad? Well, let's be honest, most Americans do (hell-o, thirty-five percent adult obesity rate...), but people born on this date *really* have a hard time when it comes to their emotions clouding their health. Read this aloud: "I am not hungry/thirsty/in need of intravenous drugs *(choose one or more)*. I am just consuming to fill a void in my life." There, you're fixed. You're welcome.

⚡AUGUST 12

On August 12, 2013, a 60-foot-wide sinkhole in Florida randomly swallowed part of a Disney resort. The ground just opened up and inhaled a large, three-story building. People born on August 12 have a sinkhole that literally lives inside of them. They are artistic by nature, and can be very charismatic, but the craving to just totally check out emotionally and abuse drugs and alcohol can be really strong... and with addiction comes near-total destruction. Consider pouring your energy into religion instead.

⚡ AUGUST 13

When the time is at nine-fifteen, the hands of the clock form a straight line stretching across its face, straight as an arrow, and that's a good analogy for someone born on August 13. You're a strong communicator, a valuable member of your family and circle of friends, and you often work in a creative field. Your lack of financial confidence is a real downer, though. More like a six-thirty.

⚡ AUGUST 14

Being around people born on August 14 is like being around a perpetual toddler. Their behavior, while almost always charming and fun, can be perplexing and might seem random. They hate to do things for themselves and prefer to be waited on hand and foot. They probably have a hard time holding down a job, unless they got a lucky break into a career where they get to call all the shots. If you are dating someone who was born on August 14, the best thing to do is just treat them like a child: hide veggies inside their favorite dishes, give them an allowance for doing chores, and tolerate their tantrums.

⚡ AUGUST 15

People born on this day tend to be very egotistical and chalk their failures up to bad luck or the roll of the dice. Their successes, on the other hand, they claim completely and like to talk about how they predicted the good fortune all along. They often have messy relationships with their families until they have children of their own, at which point they want everything to instantly repair itself after years of tension.

⚡AUGUST 16

You know how Steve Carell, star of *The Office* (US version) television series and many big-screen comedy movies, often plays a character who is straight-faced and often unaware of the humor and chaos that follow in his wake? Carell was born on August 16 and exemplifies the tendency of people born on this day to create a public alter-ego that is surprisingly different from who they consider to be their "real" self. Their secret, "true" self is reserved for only their true love, and—*spoiler alert*—their "real" self is usually pretty terrible, with questionable hygiene.

⚡AUGUST 17

"Are you talkin' to me? Are *you* talkin' to *me*?" A piece of advice for people born on August 17... Before you end up like Robert De Niro's notorious character in *Taxi Driver*, you should work on your stress management. August 17th natives, like De Niro himself, tend to have issues handling stressful situations. If their stress gets out of hand, it can affect this Leo's health and decision-making.

⚡AUGUST 18

Here's a tip if you know someone born on August 18. Make frequent dinner dates and then "forget" to bring your wallet. These Leos will foot the bill each time, quite happily, and forget all about it before your next meal. Money is not their strong suit, and they love going out and spending time with friends so much that they often put themselves in the poor house through excessive social extravagance. Don't expect much flattery from someone born on this date, though. They will say it like it is, sometimes being honest to a fault, but who really cares as long as they're paying...?

AUGUST 19

People born on this date have an appetite for life. They are successful in their careers, usually getting work that they find earnestly interesting, and they love to spend their money on the things they really want. They are hedonistic and have a tendency to get obese after they hit middle-age, if they're not already.

AUGUST 20

If you were born on August 20, chances are you have a closet full of skeletons. Probably not actual skeletons, like Erik and Lyle Menendez, who killed their parents on August 20, but figurative skeletons. You've definitely lied to significant others about how many people you've slept with, your driver's license absolutely doesn't bear your correct weight, and most likely there is a whole host of other lies that started as "white lies" and ended up painting you into a corner of dishonesty.

AUGUST 21

August 21st-er, when you walk through the mall or a department store, do you get all flushed and excited? Sometimes you just *have* to have it! The problem is... you *have* to have too much. The things that you buy are holding you prisoner, both by the drain on your bank account every time you gleefully exclaim, *"Charge it!!"* and by the sheer volume of *stuff* that you're accumulating. Get yourself back on track by watching

133

a season of *Hoarders*. You don't want to end up like the lady who found a sad litter of kittens underneath her piles of garbage, do you?

AUGUST 22

Lions born on August 22 don't flaunt their pride in the same way that other Leos do. They are suspicious and nervous, and not likely to let people into their hearts and their personal space. If you were born on this date, being alone is where you are able to find your "happy place" and channel your energy into something productive. Your mind works in surprising and often troubling ways—and you're in good company. Science fiction writer Ray Bradbury was born on August 22, as was the witty, wry Dorothy Parker. Comedienne and actress Kristin Wiig shares this birthday as well.

LEO–VIRGO CUSP

If your birthday falls between August 20 and August 23, you were born on the Leo-Virgo cusp. You sometimes feel like you have multiple personalities, with one friendly, social character coming out when you are with friends or family, and a darker, more serious side that surfaces when you're drinking alone with the shades drawn. Consider getting a pet or a roommate!

VEXED VIRGO

AUGUST 23 TO SEPTEMBER 22

Have you ever wondered why the astrological sign for people with birthdays between August 24 and September 23 is the virgin? Why, oh why, would this sign be represented by someone who is untouched and unloved in the physical sense? Bad news: being a virgin is not necessarily by choice for the great astrological maiden in the sky, though she might try to convince you that it is. She might even believe it herself. Sorry to say, the simple truth is that Virgos are kind of intense and off-putting.

Inviting a Vexed Virgo into your house is slightly like inviting in a critical mother-in-law who has been up all night on some illegal appetite-suppressants. The Virgo will start cleaning immediately. It will start with little things, like a piece of dog hair on the couch, and—if you let it—it will quickly spiral to a full-on scrubbing of the oven. All the while, Virgo will be muttering little well-intentioned insults like, "It's incredible how many dishes someone who doesn't really cook can acquire," or, "It's so nice that you feel so comfortable with me as a friend that you can invite me over when your house is in such disrepair." It's quite charming. The upside is that it's an almost-free cleaning service, with the only cost being your self-esteem.

The other upside of inviting a Virgo to your home is that they are loyal, sympathetic, charitable pals. They are true-blue and genuinely care about their friends and family. They listen to problems and offer insightful advice after a careful analysis of your situation, and also make excellent designated drivers if you can stand to have them around. They have likely calculated exactly how much they can drink per hour to stay underneath the legal limit, so you'll *usually* be safe with a Virgo behind the wheel. They also make good bar trivia partners because they are able to mentally file away and recall a lot of mostly useless information.

Whatever you do, when you're spending time with a Virgo, please don't let on that you have noticed their annoying habits. They have a tendency to freak out, and when they lose it, they'll start listing every single thing you've ever done to them. They'll remember the time that you left a coffee ring on their antique teak table because you refused to use a coaster, and the time that you brought home low-fat yogurt instead of fat-free yogurt. So bite your tongue unless you want a blow-by-blow recollection of the time that you accidentally backed your car into the garbage can.

LOVE AND RELATIONSHIPS WITH VEXED VIRGO

Who needs heat in the bedroom? It's so overrated, and what really matters is how you can work together as a team and accomplish great, non-sexy things. You could paint the bedroom furniture, for example. Or rearrange your books in alphabetical order, or—if your Virgo is feeling wild—in order of the colors of their spines. That would be equally as fun as a roll in the hay. (Note: a Virgo would never roll in hay—far too messy!).

It's important to Virgos to see good habits in their mates. You have to brush your teeth, for example, and you absolutely must keep your fingernails and toenails neatly clipped. Your skin should be clear and clean, and don't eat anything that causes an upset stomach. Virgos do not like unpleasant tummy grumbles or the disagreeable odors that are bound to follow. It all just seems so untidy and uncouth. And if you really want to drive a Virgo insane, do things like wear mismatched socks or don't change your motor oil on time.

If you can break through a Virgo's perfectionist force field and actually start a meaningful relationship with him or her, there are actually things you might enjoy in store for you. Game nights, for example, could be a lot of fun. Try *Trivial Pursuit* or *Scene It* or *Outburst!*—games where your Virgo can show off their wit and beat all their friends fair and square. You'll also enjoy meaningful conversations with a Virgo, dine on delicious, meticulously prepared meals, and your house will never be a total disaster with a Virgo at the helm. It's a pretty good deal for most of the astrological signs, though there are some signs that could never settle down and share an orderly life with a Virgo.

CHECKLIST FOR DATING A VEXED VIRGO

You'll need at least half of these things in order to have a successful relationship with a Virgo.

Manners, grammar, and social grace: If you can't at least fake these things, you'll never get past a first date with a Virgo.

Patience: Virgos are unlikely to jump into the bedroom with anyone, and even if they do, sexual compatibility may take a little while to develop.

Confidence: Virgos can be so critical that someone without confidence would shrivel in their sights.

Good conversation skills: A little sense of humor, a little knowledge about the world. Pick up a newspaper before your date with a Virgo, or—if you're under fifty years of age—do a little YouTubing and check up on Facebook for some relevant material.

Some sort of life strategy: You don't have to have a ten-year-plan necessarily (although that would be a bonus), but you should at least have a plan for your day and some sort of goal for the future.

A sense of modesty and decorum: Don't dress too flashy or wear too much jewelry or too much perfume. Impress a Virgo with good taste and reserved class. Button-up that button you were thinking about unbuttoning.

VEXED VIRGO COMPATIBILITY

VIRGO AND ARIES LOVE

If Aries ever needs help around the house, or maybe an assistant for paperwork, or any other sort of menial labor, a relationship with a Virgo could be a really profitable thing, since Virgo has a giving nature. But Virgo will definitely be shocked and a little incensed at how Aries just floats through life without a plan.

VIRGO AND TAURUS LOVE

This is a pretty solid match. A Virgo and a Taurus can look forward to red-hot date nights weighing up the merits of eggshell white versus soft ivory paint at The Home Depot—and sweet, sexy mornings debating what brand of coffee is the most environmentally responsible. Sizzling!

VIRGO AND GEMINI LOVE

Gemini is up for anything, wants to experience everything, and wants to slow down for no one. Virgo wants to stay at home and make lists of the pros and cons of each activity that Gemini suggests. Plus, it's very likely that Gemini will give Virgo a sexually transmitted disease.

VIRGO AND CANCER LOVE

"It's not *what* you said... it's *how* you said it." Practice saying this with varying levels of bitterness, anger, frustration, and sarcasm... and you'll be prepared for a merging of Virgo and Cancer. Cancer has fast, dramatic mood shifts, and the slightest thing can set Virgo off like a line of irritable dominos.

VIRGO AND LEO LOVE

Virgo and Leo both think that the massive problems in their relationship are temporary... just a bump on the road of a happy relationship. They're wrong—the fights will never stop. Leo wants his or her ego to be stroked and Virgo just wants to pick Leo apart like a vulture psychologist, chewing and analyzing every single morsel until they find out just what makes Leo behave in that cocky, proud way of theirs. A Leo feels constantly on the defensive around a Virgo, and is hesitant to let his or her guard down. It's kind of a sad match.

VIRGO AND VIRGO LOVE

Imagine for a moment one tiny Japanese bonsai tree sitting patiently on a table. Imagine a Virgo, the ideal groom for such a noble little tree, picking up a pair of small shears and beginning to snip away, very carefully, analyzing each move. Then imagine a second

Virgo hovering over the first, telling the groom what to do, reaching for the shears, repositioning the tree, criticizing each and every move... let's just say it's very likely that the shears will end up in an eyeball at the climax of this scenario.

VIRGO AND LIBRA LOVE

To Virgo, Libra is spineless and wishy-washy. To Libra, Virgo can be mean, antisocial, and unforgivably prissy. Not a recommended match. If you go for it anyway, keep to your own circles of friends because none of your pals will be able to tolerate your mate.

VIRGO AND SCORPIO LOVE

Scorpios have a purpose. They rally around causes and genuinely care about stuff. Virgos mainly just like to criticize everything and will continue to do so even if there's no positive outcome. Scorpio will soon see Virgo's global critique as complete and total neurosis rather than purposeful criticism.

VIRGO AND SAGITTARIUS LOVE

The Devil's in the details... or so a Sagittarius thinks. Virgo will drive Sagittarius to pull out all the hairs on their head with all the spreadsheets, the charts, the graphs, and diagrams... Too much, Virgo, take a step back!

VIRGO AND CAPRICORN LOVE

The sad trombone song might play every time a Virgo and Capricorn make out, but other than that it's a great match. These two signs will drive each other to achieve and strategize and amass a large reference library with titles such as *Who Stole My Cheese?* and *How to Win Friends and Influence People.*

VIRGO AND AQUARIUS LOVE

Here's a sneaky peek into the strangely formal and surprisingly incompatible Virgo-Aquarius bedroom: "Pardon me, would you mind putting your hand on my—er, no, that's not quite right... How about I reach around this side and slip my hand under—ouch, that's not comfortable either. Could you just... Oh, would you rather just watch Netflix instead?"

VIRGO AND PISCES LOVE

If Virgo can figure out how to see past the dirty socks hanging from the lampshade and the sink full of dirty dishes, and if Pisces can learn to make do with Virgo always needing to have a plan and always worrying about everything, these two might be able to make it work.

CAREER AND MONEY FOR VEXED VIRGO

You know that kid in school who, whenever group work was assigned, always just started taking notes like crazy and eventually just did the whole project and carried the slackers through. Bet you that kid was a Virgo. In the workplace, it's not that Virgos mind group work—it's more that they see the group as just another problem that they have to solve; another obstacle they must figure out a way around. When you find yourself working with a Virgo, it's best to update them—frequently—in short sentences with proper grammar, then follow up regularly... or just stay out of their way so they can do your share of the work as well and make you look good.

If you decide you can stand Virgo's annoyingly over-analytical and perfectionist ways and choose to offer them a job, make sure you're prepared to harness the Virgo and use their nit-picking for good and not evil. Keep them busy with excessive, meticulous paperwork, and volunteer activities such as the party-planning committee. Otherwise, they'll just walk around the office criticizing the quality of the cubicle dividers, the industrial carpet, and the contents of the break-room vending machine. Virgos are generally not great for raising office moral. They are very demanding and may raise the standards of a workplace and make everyone—colleagues, students, interns, or even superiors—up their game, which could be good or bad considering how much of a go-getter you are.

For employers with an exploitative streak, looking to really suck maximum above-and-beyond productivity out of minimum wages and benefits, a Virgo would be a good hire. With an occasional compliment to make sure they feel appreciated, you can practically run even the most highly skilled Virgos like sweatshop employees. In fact, send them home with your personal taxes, too, and have them drop off your dry cleaning. Virgos love to solve other peoples' problems and feel that they are irreplaceable.

ABSOLUTE WORST JOBS FOR A VEXED VIRGO

Prostitute or exotic dancer: Virgo is not bringing sexy back. Virgos can mimic human sexuality by studying books, pamphlets, and documentaries, but they're not really sexual innovators or masters of seduction. Better to leave the prostituting to Librans or Sagittarians.

Sculptor or writer: Virgos can be creative, but they need to know the parameters of a project when they begin in order to complete it to the excellent standards they expect from themselves. Subjective work such as writing or sculpting can stop Virgos in their tracks, getting them hung up on a single word or the perfectly spherical shape of a nipple or earlobe. Note: if a Virgo does end up in a subjective career in the fine arts, they'll probably develop a drinking problem and possibly require hospitalization at some point.

Public relations manager for a celebrity: Again, Virgos like to know what to expect so that they can master the task, and a PR manager for a real housewife or Miley Cyrus would never know what insanity was coming their way. Having to put a positive spin on bad behavior could also really annoy a Virgo. Critical by nature, Virgos may have a hard time swallowing their judgment and focusing on the positives when they witness shady shenanigans taking place.

JOBS THAT A VEXED VIRGO MIGHT NOT SCREW UP

Maid: If you are hiring a maid, basically the only reference you need to check is their Sun sign. If he or she is a Virgo, go for it. Virgos are fastidious and tidy and genuinely dislike clutter and disorder. They will clean your house like it's their own. You will be able to eat off the floors, though a Virgo would definitely judge you for doing something so gross as eating off the floors.

Tax auditor: Virgos don't mean to be terrible, nit-picky people, but since they tend to be terrible and nit-picky by nature, they may as well take the jobs that other astrological signs wouldn't touch with a ten-foot pole. Like tax auditor. Virgos can crunch the numbers, deliver the bad news, and are excellent at holding people accountable to standards.

Doctor: Virgos like to learn the facts, make a plan, and execute that plan. A job as a physician, surgeon, or nutritionist will allow a Virgo to apply their knowledge in a forward-thinking manner. They also excel at creating milestones for regular check-ups and can adjust the plan to meet their goals. Plus, if you need someone to clean the operating room after a surgeon has messed it up, you can always ask your Virgo doctor to help wipe everything down.

STARS OF THE SIGN VEXED VIRGO

One thing you'll notice as we compile a list of famous Vexed Virgos is that these are incredibly hard-working and industrious individuals. They became stars by virtue of their rigorous work and strategic decisions. Very few Virgos get a free ride on the fame train. Musicians like Michael Jackson and Beyoncé Knowles began performing as toddlers, and Pink was singing her insane little heart out on stage by the time she hit adolescence. Two of the stars of the British band One Direction are hard-working Virgos (Niall and Liam), and Jennifer Hudson shows off her industry not only with singing success, but also with a slimmed-down silhouette after whittling her pear shape into an hour-glass.

There are also an abnormally large number of American Virgo television talk-show hosts, including Jimmy Fallon, Dr. Phil McGraw, Regis Philbin, Dr. Drew, Bill O'Reilly, and Ricki Lake! This is probably because Virgos have the ability to drill down to the crux of issues gracefully; they're analytical by nature, and while their manners do prevent them from being too pushy (excluding Bill O'Reilly, of course), they can tactfully work the truth out of a guest by asking clever questions.

A down side of the structure and strategy of the Virgo is that when it's used for evil... it can be very evil. A Virgo is not distracted by romance or frivolity, and therefore has plenty of time to plan and execute terrible things. Jesse James, the famous Missouri outlaw who robbed banks with his brother, was a Virgo. James was also known to be a good father, which just goes to show you how adept Virgos are at finding successful work-life balances. Similarly, family man Carlo Gambino (the real-life *Godfather*) was also able to blend his family activities with his nine-to-five hands-on crime commitments.

VEXED VIRGO BIRTHDAYS

⚡ LEO–VIRGO CUSP
If your birthday falls between August 20 and August 23, you were born on the Leo-Virgo cusp, and chances are you sometimes feel like you are hiding your true self from others. You could reveal your inner self by

revealing your feelings—but you should probably just continue the charade because other people are more comfortable with the fake version of you.

⚡ AUGUST 23

Everyone loves you, August 23rd! They love the way you wag your tail when you're excited, the way you sit and stay when you're told, the way you play, and especially the way you greet everyone with a big, warm kiss. You might not be the sharpest tool in the shed, but you're very well loved.

⚡ AUGUST 24

How are you feeling? You look kind of run down. Just tired? If you were born on August 24, you might be a hypochondriac—and your cheeks definitely look flushed. It also may be difficult for you to show your emotions about anything but your make-believe ailments. Why don't you stop shining a flashlight down your throat and hug your significant other instead?

⚡ AUGUST 25

Ivan the Terrible was born on this day in 1530, along with evil tyrants from other walks of life: Sean Connery, Tim Burton, Regis Philbin, and Rachael Ray. When people who have this birthday overcome their native anxiety and discover what they want to do with their lives, watch out! A freight train won't be able to stop them.

⚡ AUGUST 26

The genesis of the most boring, do-gooder Virgos— bearing in mind that Virgos might be the most boring, do-gooder sign of the entire zodiac—is August 26. You

work hard toward your goals. You love your family and friends. You care about the world and try to make it a better place. Who do you think you are, Mother Teresa? A lady who, by the way, was born on August 26.

⚡ AUGUST 27

Stop. Freaking. Out. If you were born on August 27, try to just relax, as you lie in bed awake at night, thinking about everything you have to do the next day. Your family probably won't starve. You probably won't screw up your presentation too badly. An ax murderer probably won't break into your house. Whatever you do, don't lie awake and think about the fact that you share your birthday with Ed Gein, the serial killer who inspired not one, not two, but *three* blockbuster horror movie villains (Norman Bates, Jame Gumb, and Leatherface). Seriously, can you see what too much anxiety and not enough sleep can do to a body? Take a chill-pill!

⚡ AUGUST 28

Look around, August 28th-er! You might notice that all of your friends are more talented than you are. Don't be jealous! It's a good thing, and the fact that these geniuses tolerate the likes of you means that you must bring something to the table. Do you make a mean potato salad? Are you particularly promiscuous? Whatever you're doing, keep it up, so that the invitations keep on coming!

⚡ AUGUST 29

People born on August 29 often believe that money is just stuff you trade for things you want. Like Michael Jackson, who was born on this day, who just wanted to own an amusement park and wild jungle animals and get reconstructive plastic surgery. Simple dreams for a simple man born on a simple day in August.

⚡ AUGUST 30

Most Virgos are concerned with health and exercise, but those born on August 30 tend to be a little more luscious. They really adore food—not only its nutritional qualities, but also its sensuality and flavor. For people born on this day, junk food might become a problem, and that might lead to spandex pants, which might in turn lead to having to buy two seats on the airplane, which is actually fine because it means that you'll get two bags of peanuts.

⚡ AUGUST 31

Maria Montessori, founder of the Montessori schools (a chain of very expensive, private early education schools that teach entitled children how to pursue their dreams rather than churn them through the meat grinder of public education), is a perfect example of someone born on August 31. You see how everyone else does it, decide it's not good enough, and then—no matter the odds—you find a way to force your creative ideas and goodwill on everyone else.

⚡ SEPTEMBER 1

It took a lot to get you where you are, September 1st native. Your great-grandparents' decisions impacted on your grandparents' decisions, and your parents' decisions put you in the shoes in which you stand. You always do the best you can, but you'll have to realize that sometimes that's just not good enough to impress your parents, grandparents, and great-grandparents. Forget 'em.

⚡ SEPTEMBER 2

Once bitten, twice shy... and you are a shy one, aren't you? Did someone hurt you? Did someone, maybe a close friend or an early love interest, break your heart? You are emotionally damaged goods, plain and simple, and that can deeply impact your ability to love again. If you do fill the void with friends or lovers, you'll constantly be comparing them to people in your past. It might just be better to give up and get several cats.

⚡ SEPTEMBER 3

Not everything in life is a competition, unless you were born on September 3. For those people, everything seems like a race, whether it's professional achievements or how many Facebook friends or Twitter followers you can amass, or how perfect your family looks around your dinner table at a home-cooked meal. The ultra-competitive Charlie Sheen, who was born on this day, pronounced himself the "winner."

⚡ SEPTEMBER 4

On September 4, 2006, Steve Irwin, better known as the Crocodile Hunter, died suddenly when attacked by a stingray while snorkeling. It was a dark day for fans, though deadly jungle animals across the globe rejoiced. What does this have to do with people who are born on September 4, you may ask? Well, like people who pursue professional crocodile hunting, September 4th-ers might find themselves shirking a normal punch-the-clock-type job and looking for something a little off the beaten path. They want to make their own way professionally, and sometimes ignore the valid concerns of their friends and family in order to do it.

⚡ SEPTEMBER 5

If you were born on September 5, stand up right now and walk to a mirror. You probably look pretty well put together, right? Even if you're in your pajamas, they aren't paint-stained or torn, and your hair's not totally out of control. And you're probably multitasking right now, as you read this book, toward self-improvement—maybe whitening your teeth or setting your hair with curlers? Well, good for you. Except for that one, super-dark secret that no one knows about, you're practically perfect in every way. Better keep a lid on it.

⚡ SEPTEMBER 6

"For unto us, a child is born..." Chapter 9, Verse 6 of Isaiah—kind of a famous one if you're into Biblical references. If you, in fact, *are* a child born on 9-6, you might not be as Christlike as one would hope. In fact, you are probably not very disciplined, and slightly greedy when it comes to food and possessions.

⚡ SEPTEMBER 7

Grandma Moses was born in New York on September 7. She didn't start painting until she was in her 70s, and her paintings became collector's pieces all over the globe. People born on September 7 tend to not find their callings until later in life, like Grandma Moses did. Unfortunately, most people won't become famous worldwide and live to over one hundred years old, so if you want to hurry it up and expedite your journey of self-discovery, that's probably for the best.

⚡ SEPTEMBER 8

What doesn't kill you makes you stronger. At least, this is what people born on September 8 tell themselves when they do dumb things and learn painful lessons. People born on this day tend to view their spouse as a pal instead of a lover, leading to good teamwork everywhere but the bedroom.

⚡ SEPTEMBER 9

9-9 is a nice, square day for nice, square Virgos. There are nine innings in baseball, nine months in a pregnancy, and the number nine is revered in Hinduism. Virgos born on this day are complete perfectionists and get frustrated with imperfections in both themselves and others. If this happens, go play a game of nine-ball and drink at least nine beers to settle down!

⚡ SEPTEMBER 10

If you were born on September 10, you likely have a full stable of friends that you secretly resent. You don't want their patronizing advice, their annoyingly chummy conversation, but somehow they're always buzzing around you. It's because you have this inexplicable magnetism and charisma, and even though you would rather be alone most of the time, you can't be because these people keep on a-coming back. Gnats, the lot of them.

⚡ SEPTEMBER 11

You've probably gotten the reaction more times than you can count... the grimace followed by a *cluck* and slow head shake that comes along with sharing your date of birth with a new acquaintance. People born on September 11 care deeply about others' feelings, so chances are you often end up comforting the person who asked and reassuring them that everything will be okay. The good news is that your friends and family will probably never forget your birthday, and everyone will rally around you with excellent presents to make up for the awkwardness.

⚡ SEPTEMBER 12

Close your eyes and think back to your childhood, September 12th-er. Was it all picket fences and pies on windowsills? Trips to the mall with your family, with a stop at TGI Fridays on the way home? You have the strangest, rose-colored glasses of all time... because your childhood actually sucked, like everyone else's, but for some reason you remember it to be the absolute epitome of wholesomeness. This is cute for you, but actually slightly destructive for any offspring you might have, who will be forced to try to recreate these faux memories. Luckily, you're financially stable and can save up for lots of therapeutic help.

⚡ SEPTEMBER 13

If you were born this day, you may be kind of a lone wolf. You're nervous and don't have even the minimal social grace that Virgos usually have. You probably do a strange job, maybe one that you enjoy despite its low status or uncommon hours. Roald Dahl, author of eccentric children's classics such as *Charlie and the Chocolate Factory* and *Matilda*, was born on this day... as was the chocolate magnate Milton Hershey, who may very likely have been Dahl's model for the wild Willy Wonka. Both of these successful men worked tirelessly at jobs they loved and produced strange and beautiful works, so keep at it. Your sock puppet theater or self-published moustache-grooming handbook will take off if you just persevere a little while longer.

⚡ SEPTEMBER 14

If you were born on September 14, you are so self-righteous that people can barely stand you! There's not much more to say. Be nicer to the people who do stand you and try to put your ideals on the back burner so that you can genuinely connect with others.

⚡ SEPTEMBER 15

When the time is at nine-fifteen, the hands of the clock form a straight line stretching across its face, straight as an arrow, and that's a good analogy for someone born on September 15. You're a strong communicator, a valuable member of your family and circle of friends, and often work in a creative field. Your lack of financial confidence is a real downer, though. More like a six-thirty.

⚡ SEPTEMBER 16

People born on September 16 might be the cheesiest, most earnest people in the entire zodiac. They are genuinely spiritual (not just faking it on Sunday mornings), and when they meet new people they actually feel like their lives have changed, usually for the better. Being with someone born on September 16 is like walking through a meadow and enjoying each cloud, each flower, and each little bird song. It's sickeningly touching.

⚡ SEPTEMBER 17

September 17th-ers expect—nay, *demand*—stability in all the people around them. If this is your birthday, you don't want to take risks because—oh no—you might not be able to predict the outcome exactly. You're also incredibly stubborn, which can frustrate those around you. Loosen up.

⚡ SEPTEMBER 18

If you were born on September 18, you could be pretty difficult to trust. People have a hard time knowing what to expect from you. You fluctuate between wanting to be around people and wanting to fly solo. While you have big dreams and goals, your tendency to interpret the truth and mold it to what you want can get you in trouble. Lance Armstrong shares this Virgo birthday. Enough said.

⚡ SEPTEMBER 19

People born on this day are classy folks. They don't often burp at the dinner table, cut in line, or talk with their mouth full, and they tend to have very good personal hygiene like many other Virgos. September 19th-ers are sometimes drawn to the limelight... but it's not usually about their ego, more about their natural inner glow. Such charmers, these natives!

⚡ SEPTEMBER 20

Work, work, work. It's all people born on this day ever think about. It seems as if their families are simply there as support systems to get them to and from work. Their meals give them nutrients so that they can work more. If you want to play a funny prank on someone born on September 20, hide his or her cell phone and laptop. You could leave little clues around and send them on wild goose chases. But don't keep the jig up too long... their heads might actually explode.

⚡ SEPTEMBER 21

People born on September 21 are quaking little mice inside bodies that don't always hint at their fears. They need to be paired up in life with a personal cheerleader who can help this Virgo to put aside their worries and ignore their fear of failure. This partner should also be a nurse, as September 21st-ers are notoriously bad at taking care of their bodies and eating a healthy diet. It would also be helpful if the partner could obtain a degree in counseling, as people born on this day are often working through a lot of issues from the past. Basically, September 21st natives are total basket cases.

⚡ SEPTEMBER 22

If you were born on September 22, you are a study in extremes. You yo-yo back and forth between extremely healthy eating habits and junk food binges, and you do not feel like you fit in with your family at all. You're a loyal friend but you can be unforgiving: as soon as someone screws up, your heart is like a guillotine slamming shut, severing all ties.

⚡ VIRGO—LIBRA CUSP

If you were born between September 19th and September 23, you were born on the cusp and may have tendencies of both zodiac signs. For those born on the cusp between Virgo and Libra, they might find themselves often in the middle of arguments—and not be able to choose a side. Both sides seem valid and reasonable. People born on this day may find that their inability to choose makes them nervous, and really lousy companions on date nights. "Oh I don't know, where do *you* want to go?"

LOUSY LIBRA
SEPTEMBER 23 TO OCTOBER 23

How do you confuse a Libra? Don't worry about it, they're already confused. The astrological symbol for Libra is the scales, tipping back and forth, back and forth, constantly weighing every decision, analyzing the ups and downs, twisting all the choices around and around and around until... enough already! Just make a decision, Libra. C'mon.

Another thing about Libras: they're bandwagon-jumpers. If you're a Libra and reading this, look down. You have those shoes that you read about online, right? And those new pants that are all the rage. You're probably looking pretty spiffy down to your toenail polish, jewelry, hair products, moisturizer, or cologne. Congratulations, trendster. Looking good.

Oh, and for sure your Libra friend liked that band *before* it was cool (they actually probably did, as infuriating as that is). But don't call them out on being trendy, because Libras really, really want you to like them, and they worry a lot about what everybody else thinks.

157

Psst. Here's what everyone else thinks: Libras are a little bit pretentious. They would argue you to the death that the difference between teal and aquamarine is vitally important for anyone who claims to know their colors, but for the record, not many others really give a damn about subtle nuance the way that a Libran does. They're the same way about issues of injustice, of right or wrong, or the atrocity of white pants after Labor Day—and like to discuss these issues *ad nauseum*.

Other astrological signs are definitely jealous of a Libra's effortless ability to put together an outfit, or a dinner party, or whatever it is they're working on at any given moment, because they always nail it. Libras have a elegance, style, and social grace, and the party doesn't really start until they arrive. But don't tell them that. Seriously. They'll get all proud of themselves and you'll never hear the end of it.

LOVE AND RELATIONSHIPS WITH LOUSY LIBRA

If you've fallen in love with a Libra, know two things. First, you've got your work cut out for you. Libras demand to be courted, entertained—wooed, if you will—at least at the beginning. Helpful hint: opals and pearls are the birthstones of Librans, so if you get a chance to run by the jewelry store before taking a Libra out on a date, it might be a quicker path to the bedroom. Don't worry, eventually the Libra's loyal side will come out and the two of you can get old and fat in peace, eating your potato chips on the couch and surfing the web on matching laptops.

The second thing you should know if you fall in love with a Libra is you're probably not alone. Libras often string several romantic partners along at any given time because of their inability to choose. A lot of times they don't even know they're doing it and just rack up a bunch of poor lovestruck fools in their noble effort to find their true love.

The trend-jumping side of Libras comes out in their relationships, too, and before you know it a Libra who is afraid of heights will claim that they love rock climbing, or a devout vegetarian will decide to order bacon-wrapped beef tripe just to impress you. Because they are constantly weighing everything back and forth, don't be surprised if they switch it up on you when you least expect it. They have such a hard time making decisions, in fact, that they will likely enlist the help of their friends, their crazy family, a psychic, and a therapist before committing to anything. Make way for the peanut gallery—your life will be mob ruled if you hook up with a Libran.

And another thing—Libras are *always* keeping score. They'll repay, tit for tat, the exact amount of effort they perceive that you're putting into the relationship. This includes the cost of gifts, the thoughtfulness of a gesture, and the amount of *oomph* in the bedroom. This is to say, if your relationship with a Libra sucks, it's probably time to look in the mirror.

CHECKLIST FOR DATING A LOUSY LIBRA

You'll need at least half of these things in order to have a successful relationship with a Libra.

Really good health insurance: this should include all manner of health care, including therapy, massage, and manicures (if possible).

Stylish clothes, accessories, jewelry, shoes, etc:. But don't overshadow your Libra. Check out their style and then take it down by half a notch—so they're proud to be with you in public, but not intimidated by your swagger.

A short-term memory problem: It's better if you just don't try to remember what they said last week, instead of trying to keep up with their changing tides.

Knowledge of all things trendy and cultured: Know where the hottest club is and name-drop it. Get a table at the coolest restaurant. Box seats to a theater production? Good. Private art museum tour? Better. Exclusive invitations to red carpet events? Yeah, you're golden.

Decisiveness: Make decisions for your Libra ahead of time, and give them plenty of notice, so they don't lose their confused little minds.

LOUSY LIBRA COMPATIBILITY

LIBRA AND ARIES LOVE

Take it slow, Aries. Libra needs time to obnoxiously weigh all of the pros and cons of dating you. Long-term relationship success is unlikely but if you get a chance to hook up, sparks will probably fly in the bedroom.

LIBRA AND TAURUS LOVE

Don't do it. First, Taurus is practical and likes to be in control but Libra doesn't really dig that. If you do get together, please immediately find out where you can buy a padded room and a full-body suit made out of bubblewrap, because your constant fights might get a little rowdy.

LIBRA AND GEMINI LOVE

Yes, yes, *yes!!* That's an impression of Libra and Gemini in the bedroom... when they're sixty-eight. Because they'll still be married to each other, and getting each other's rocks off.

LIBRA AND CANCER LOVE

There is so much to fight about it's almost not worth it. Cancer's moody and Libra's sure to annoy them with their constant analyzing. Libra's extravagant and Cancer's critical. How 'bout you just stay friends? Like, without benefits, because Cancer can't really bring it the way Libra wants it. No offense, Cancer. Libra's just too high maintenance for you.

LIBRA AND LEO LOVE

There's the possibility for long-term love here, if Libra and Leo can just meet up in the bedroom whenever a disagreement arrives.

LIBRA AND VIRGO LOVE

Libra demands to go out with friends, spend money, and be wooed. Virgo is all, "nah, let's stay home and count our money." If you can get past that—over, and over, and over again—it could work. Sounds fun.

LIBRA AND LIBRA LOVE

This relationship could go on way longer than necessary because no one wants to talk about the elephant in the room. Group dates are often more successful than one-on-one romance, and this could be a very expensive love affair as each person tries to match the other's extravagance.

LIBRA AND SCORPIO LOVE

You know those couples on talk shows that cheat on each other, accuse someone else of being the baby's daddy, fight, scratch, and despise each other, but always end up back together? Most of them are probably Libra-Scorpio connections.

LIBRA AND SAGITTARIUS LOVE

Sagittarius will definitely keep Libra occupied with their adventure-seeking and clever conversation. The main problem here is that Sagittarius does not want to be pinned down and will fight Libra—kicking and screaming—for independence.

LIBRA AND CAPRICORN LOVE

I ain't sayin' Libra's a gold digger, but Capricorn could really turn a Libra on with their pursuit of riches. The problem is Capricorn will be out busting his or her hump while Libra's lounging around with their friends all the time. Libra better find an interesting way to make it up to Capricorn. Cue the music, dim the lights...

LIBRA AND AQUARIUS LOVE

This is one of the best matches Libra could have. Aquarius is a little more stubborn, Libra's a little more trendy and spendy, but overall these two could tolerate each other.

LIBRA AND PISCES LOVE

Libra meets Pisces. They adore each other for about two minutes until Pisces starts whining about the world and saying snide things about Libra's idiotic friends and Libra's stupid hobbies. Libra suggests that Pisces gets a life. Pisces threatens suicide. Luckily, both signs like to end fights with hot sex, so at least it will be fun.

CAREERS AND MONEY FOR LOUSY LIBRA

Libras are not good at menial, physical labor. It's not that they're incapable of, say, lifting heavy boxes on an assembly line in a messy factory, but they just get bored so fast that they start to whine about it and don't shut up until happy hour. That said, you don't really want a Libra much further up the corporate ladder in a high leadership role, because they can be wishy-washy about decisions. If you've accidentally hired a Libra, the upside is that many are good at working in teams and can handle conflicts with diplomacy and tact.

If you're trying to get maximum productivity from a Libra in the workplace, you'll need to get organized— and have a big budget. First, hire an interior designer to paint the walls in soothing, complementary colors. Then, get an ergonomics expert to come in and adjust all the chairs or yoga balls or whatever the kids are sitting on these days. Lastly, make sure to limit distractions. Maybe pull some blinds down over windows that have a good view. Consider turning off the phones, blocking Facebook and Twitter, and screening emails. Oh, and put moderately interesting art up on the walls. If it's too interesting, they'll spend all day looking at it, but if there's no art, they'll feel uncomfortable and itchy.

Did you know that within a few years, lawyers will outnumber human beings on the planet? Chances are quite a few of those lawyers will be Librans. Librans are drawn to the law because of its sense of fairness, of justice, equality for all, and—most importantly—the cold, hard cash. Libras can be high maintenance and a big paycheck will help them live their fancy-schmancy lifestyle.

ABSOLUTE WORST JOBS FOR LOUSY LIBRA

Investigative Journalist: Libras really should be shielded from the information that life isn't fair. Their purpose in life is to balance things, and when Libras find out that the rich just keep getting richer, and that really terrible things happen to adorable children and puppies, it is very upsetting for them. Ignorance is bliss.

Accountant: It's not that Libras aren't bright enough to work with numbers... it's just that they're distracted by more interesting things. Pretty, shiny things.

Admissions Officer: Hmm, do you admit the kid with the 4.0 and the volunteer work or the kid who wrote their admissions essay in poetry form? The one who excelled in sports or the one who grew up in Africa with an adopted family? This type of job would drive most Libras batty.

JOBS THAT A LOUSY LIBRA MIGHT NOT SCREW UP

Host or hostess: Because they love being the center of attention, and they usually look put together and somewhat attractive, and they are good conversationalists, you can usually trust a Libra to make guests feel at home.

Designer: You can trust a Libra to have good taste most of the time. Whether you're looking for a nice, clean website design, a nice job with interior decoration, or even decent landscaping work, a Libra will rise to the occasion. Just don't trust them to stay within the budget.

Referee: Libras want to be fair, even if it kills them. Their symbol is the scales, with each side tipping back and forth until they reach even-stevens. For this reason, Libras make decent moderators, little league referees, and judges.

STARS OF THE SIGN LOUSY LIBRA

Bonnie, of Bonnie *and Clyde*, was a Libra through and through. She vainly posed for snapshots in a fashionable dress while on the run during her crime spree, and of course she displayed the Libran loyalty by

staying with Clyde up until the last minute. The very last minute, in fact—the minute they were gunned down by police officers in a storm of bullets.

Other infamous Libras also got wrapped up in organized crime, and one can't help but wonder if Libras' collaborative nature leads them to do terrible, terrible things. Together. Sure, some Libras use their social spirit for good: Mahatma Gandhi was a Libra, as was the philosopher and religious leader Confucius and the inventor and humanist Alfred Nobel. On the other hand, the list of lousy Libras goes on and on... You've got Ma Barker, the mother and possible co-conspirator to two notorious gangsters, and Albert Anastasia, head of the *Murder, Incorporated* crew of killers that committed a speculated 900–1,000 murders in the 1930s and '40s.

Some Libras are less sociable than others. Another extra-special Libra is Beverly Allitt, a nurse in a children's ward who poisoned thirteen sick infants, murdering four of them. Bobby Joe Long preyed on solo women, raping and killing at least ten around Tampa Bay, Florida.

But not all Libras are psycho killers, *qu'est que c'est*. The amount of Libras who flaunt their theatrical nature in show business is staggering. Just a few of the A-listers born under the Libra sign are Hugh Jackman, Will Smith, Kate Winslet, Gwyneth, Paltrow and Matt Damon. Many musicians also have Libran birthdays. There's Snoop Dogg, John Lennon, and the very creepy but talented Chuck Berry, who was accused of setting up a video camera into the ladies' room of a restaurant he owned. Ew. Two other slightly creepy (but significantly less talented) Libras who show off their star signs' vanity and sense of self-importance are Kim Kardashian and Bristol Palin.

LOUSY LIBRA BIRTHDAYS

⚡ VIRGO—LIBRA CUSP

The Virgo-Libra cusp spans roughly from September 22–September 23. For people born during this 48-hour period, you may find you have tendencies of both signs. For people born on the Virgo-Libra cusp, you'll find that you're obsessed with the details. You want everything to look perfect, to smell perfect—to BE perfect. Once something has proven itself (or *him*self or *her*self) to be imperfect, you no longer have any interest in dealing with it (or him or her). Perhaps because of your perfectionism, you have lower self-confidence. Nothing ever seems good enough and there's just this overwhelming realization that everything is crap.

⚡ SEPTEMBER 23

September 23 is the birthday of ancient rulers Caesar Augustus and Kublai Khan. Both are known for their political strategizing and empire-building. Famous musicians Bruce Springsteen and Ray Charles built empires of a different sort: both stars set records for album and ticket sales in their prime. Of course you will likely never be as popular as these outliers, but have fun building your Lego® empires and performing for your cats.

⚡ SEPTEMBER 24

Your love life will not be easy if your birthday is on September 24. It just seems that something is always causing upheaval and heartache, even in stable relationships. Like when your idiot spouse leaves a

167

coffee cup on the coffee table *without* a coaster. That's clearly a personal attack on you, right? Take a deep breath and try pursuing an artistic, creative career like great September 24th-ers before you, including Jim Henson and F. Scott Fitzgerald. It could pay off, and even if it doesn't, it will at least distract you from bugging your romantic partner about every little thing.

⚡ SEPTEMBER 25

On September 25, 1978, two airplanes literally crashed into each other in the sky, mid-air, and then plummeted to the ground, killing 144 passengers. Just like the pilots of these two planes, who missed all the signals that would have prevented the collision, your friends and family might miss the subtle hints that you drop to convey your true feelings, if this is your birthday. You have a tendency to expect a lot from yourself and from others, but are pretty bad at communicating those expectations. Work on it.

⚡ SEPTEMBER 26

Do you, September 26 native, ever have deep, dark, violent thoughts? If so, you'd be in good company with others born on this day. The "Mad Hatter," aka "Lord High Executioner," aka mobster Albert Anastasia, head of *Murder, Inc.,* was born on this day, along with the super-creepy Ronald DeFeo, of Amityville, who shot his whole family while they slept: mother, father, two sisters and two brothers. Ironically, many people born on this day have very close relationships with their siblings and family and somehow resist their urges to shoot them all.

⚡ SEPTEMBER 27

"Scrappy" is a word often used to describe those with a September 27 birthday. If this is your birthday, you are competitive, determined, and have no desire to settle down and rush into a relationship. You would prefer to draw out the chase as long as possible. Speaking of the chase, September 27 saw the end of the spiritually insightful cartoon series *Tom & Jerry*, in 2005, and marked the extinction of the majestic and ferocious Balinese tiger in 1937.

SEPTEMBER 28

Confucius say, "Happy birthday." That's right, September 28 is Confucius's birthday; the day he began collecting and slinging his simple-yet-oh-so-true nuggets of wisdom. Like Confucius, people born on September 28 have a tendency to attract many friends and devotees—almost a cult-like following. What natives of this birthdate have in charisma, they lack in patience and are prone to lose interest in a project quickly if they don't see results.

SEPTEMBER 29

People born on September 29 are sneaky. They like keeping secrets, get shifty in crowds, and rely heavily on their friends and family for emotional support when they get moody and distracted. Lucky for September 29th-ers, most of the time their loved ones are willing to help and support them. Just remember... your spouse cannot be forced to testify against you in a court of law.

SEPTEMBER 30

You're so cool and collected, September 30th native. Just look at you: perfect hair, nice smile, excellent clothes... until someone makes you angry. Then you essentially become your own version of the Hulk or Mr. Hyde. It can be really kind of nerve-wracking to be around you, especially when you set your sights on

something you want, because you'll ignore everything else to get it.

⚡ OCTOBER 1

Fun fact: on this day in 1971, Walt Disney World opened. Less fun fact: in the last ten years, something like twenty people have died during or shortly after their visit to Disney World. It's not all fun and games, people. In other news, Libras born on this day might get beat down quite a bit, but they will probably be okay. October 1st Libras have a natural resilience that makes them just keep coming back for more.

⚡ OCTOBER 2

If this is your birthday, please go check your credit card balance right now. Is it a little high? Oh my. A *lot* high? Oh dear. It's not surprising. Libras born on this day are obsessed with the finer things in life, with luxury and style. Ooh la la, Libra. The self-control factor is lacking for October 2nd Libras, and often health issues such as obesity and liver damage can arise from their overindulgence. Why fight it? Just go nuts. You'll be a burden on society in one way or another anyway, eventually.

⚡ OCTOBER 3

It's not that you don't want to be in a stable, healthy relationship—you just don't know how. Libras born on this day are constantly on the *amour* rollercoaster, falling in and out of love. On this day in 2003, Roy—of the duo Siegfried and Roy—was attacked by his beloved tiger. Eight years earlier, O.J. Simpson received his not-guilty verdict for the murder of his ex-wife Nicole Brown Simpson and Ronald Goldman. Talk about love roller coasters.

⚡ OCTOBER 4

Ten-four, good buddy. Truckers reference your birthday over CB radios as an acknowledgment of information of instructions. Like a trucker, you're kind of a rolling stone: you tend to do whatever you want to do, whenever you want to do it. And you usually get away with it, too, without getting too much static from friends and family. This kind of lifestyle can lead to great creative successes, like bestselling vampire novelist Anne Rice and hip-hop producer Russell Simmons... or to just plain loneliness, like a trucker headed northbound on an abandoned highway.

⚡ OCTOBER 5

You have a desire to *know* things and to tell your friends about those things, but you know that everyone else knows that you know... that you don't know much at all. It's probable that all your friends secretly think that you haven't had enough real-life experience to really understand some of the spiritual or political issues that you keep going on and on about in your endless jabberings. It's probable that you agree with them, when you really examine it deep down. It won't be easy but try to just *shhhhhhhhhh*, listen to what others say, and hold back the flow of the *blah-blah-blah.*

⚡ OCTOBER 6

Why is a raven like a writing desk? Lewis Carroll's Mad Hatter wore a piece of paper in his hat with "10 / 6" scrawled on it. Some say it's the size of the hat. Some say it's the price. But we know that it's actually a call-out to October 6th birthdays. Like the Mad Hatter, you can be extremely unpredictable. You fancy yourself as an artist and can totally lose yourself in fantasy. Look, there's a smiling cat sitting next to you—better go get him a cup of tea.

⚡ OCTOBER 7

On October 7, 1959, the USSR's Luna 3 beamed the first pictures of the far side of the Moon down to Earth... *You're* a little like the dark side of the Moon, aren't you, October 7th birthday boy/girl? Your true self is a little bit dark, and hidden off from the rest of the world. It's also unlikely there's any intelligent life to be found there...

⚡ OCTOBER 8

Don't freak out when you read this, but you don't handle stress well. Do you find yourself up late at night, thinking about the world's injustices small and large? Do you writhe around in your bed sheets and bite your nails down to the quick? Well, get a Xanax and stop bugging your spouse. If he or she leaves you, you'll have even more stress.

⚡ OCTOBER 9

You tend to lose touch with what *is* and idealize things, people, whole eras in history... for example, even though your childhood was a teeming mass of crazy, you remember it as being *just right*. Similarly, you imagine that there's some perfect person out there, a soul mate, someone who's going to "complete you." Your very own Yoko Ono, if you will. Side note: John Lennon *and* his son Sean Lennon both were born on October 9.

⚡ OCTOBER 10

People with October 10 birthdays think they're badasses. Some actually are, like rock star David Lee Roth, jazz king Thelonious Monk, and football god Brett Favre. Others just really think they are badasses, but can successfully veil their egos with Libra charm. October 10th-ers will take the reins of any conversation or relationship to steer it in the direction they choose, and they are ever-so-slightly power hungry.

OCTOBER 11

Good to know: October 11th is International Coming Out Day! If you've been waiting for a good time, here it is. If it's your birthday, you probably write bad poetry and need therapy. That is to say, you are confused and probably blame your parents for everything that's not quite perfect in your life. A therapist can only help so much and your book of poems will probably never get published. Good luck with that.

OCTOBER 12

The bad news is that if you're not already cheating on your significant other, you likely will cheat at some point in the near future. October 12th natives love to flirt, to meet new people, to—ahem—expand their horizons (euphemism alert). The slightly better news is that you're adorable and charming, and can probably get away with it. That doesn't make you a good person, though. Just remember that.

OCTOBER 13

You don't really trust anyone, do you? Do you get a sense of discomfort when sharing secrets, even with someone you allegedly love? It's okay, you can channel this inability to really let people in by anonymously climbing the corporate ladder to some middle-management job where you'll claim to enjoy the journey, but not the destination. Because, let's face it, the destination kind of sucks.

⚡ OCTOBER 14

Sorry to say that October 14 is cursed. Ask the Chicago Cubs. In 1908, they won a World Series on October 14, which set into motion their century-long losing streak. Also noteworthy is that several porn stars were born on October 14, including Jessica Drake and Vanessa Lane. People born on this day know how to work hard—really hard—to get ahead. Build up a sweat. Get their hands dirty. You get the picture.

⚡ OCTOBER 15

The posterchild for this birthday is Mr. Untouchable: Leroy "Nicky" Barnes worked as a crime boss who smuggled loads of drugs into NYC in the 1970s. This disco-era big shot embodied the desire of October 15th-ers to have tons of power and flashy, stylish clothes and accessories. The only lesson that other natives of October 15 can take away is *don't get caught* as you hedonistically pursue the pleasure and desire from which you are unable to restrain yourself.

⚡ OCTOBER 16

You're like a big kid. You eat like a kid, your favorite snacks are sweet and salty junk food, and you make simple comfort foods when you cook. You probably like coloring and childish games as well, and have tried out at least half a dozen careers. Just a tip: it's *not* cute to wear pigtails when you're older than thirty-three-and-a-half, so try to keep your immaturity out of your wardrobe.

⚡ OCTOBER 17

Lessons come hard to you. Stupid hard. You have to really suffer in order to absorb the wisdom that seems to come naturally to others, don't you? On October 17, 1989, California got hit with a deadly earthquake that killed fifty-seven people. Just for perspective, you'll personally have to live through your own emotional earthquake about a hundred times before remembering to duck and cover.

⚡ OCTOBER 18
Go get 'em, Tiger. You will tear out the throat of your opponent. You will out-strategize, out-analyze, and out-perform every single obstacle in your path. You don't have a lot of close friends, but that's totally your choice, right? Or could it be that people are somehow turned off by your charmingly aggressive personality? No. That can't be it.

⚡ OCTOBER 19
Controversy seems to follow you everywhere. Why is it that wherever you go, the people around you seem to be in turmoil? It's not a coincidence. Either you cause chaos by your mere presence, or you are subconsciously attracted to it. Just like how Evander Holyfield, an October 19th native, was simply minding his own business when Mike Tyson went nuts and bit off his ear. Holyfield was a completely innocent bystander.

⚡ OCTOBER 20
It's better to go out in a fiery ball of flames than to simply fade away. At least that's what the band Lynyrd Skynyrd thought when they plummeted to their deaths on October 20, 1977, in Mississippi. The crash killed lead singer Ronnie Van Zant and others on the plane. October 20 is actually a big day for musicians, both living and dead. Tom Petty and Snoop Dogg share this

birthday. Also, baseball legend Mickey Mantle, who wasn't officially recognized for his musical prowess but is rumored to be a fine whistler. So there you have it.

⚡ OCTOBER 21

Stand up and look down. Can you see your toes? If not, you're a typical October 21st native. If you can see your toes, congratulations, you've beaten the odds—but don't expect it to last. People with this birthday really dig rich foods and sweets and even though you may experience spurts of healthy eating habits, you are destined to pig out. Kim Kardashian is a famous October 21st native, as is *Star Wars* star Carrie Fisher, both of whom have publicly struggled with weight issues and conspicuous over-consumption.

⚡ OCTOBER 22

Heartbreak is the worst, and chances are you've experienced it multiple times. People with an October 22nd birthday are particularly vulnerable to getting soul-crushed by their love interests. Natives of October 22 really take the Libran quality of yo-yo dieting to an extreme with huge day-to-day shifts in eating habits and exercise routines. Watch the stretch marks if this is your birthday!

⚡ LIBRA–SCORPIO CUSP

People born on October 22–23, who fall on the Libra-Scorpio cusp, are exceedingly honest and critical. If this is your birthday, you have a tendency to pick others apart... and while you may have developed a reputation for being an honest source of feedback, you've also developed a reputation for being a total jerk.

SURLY SCORPIO

OCTOBER 24 TO NOVEMBER 22

If the Scorpion's wicked, poisonous tail is cut off through some cruel act of nature, guess what? It just grows a new one. Like their deadly-and-disgusting, astrological animal guide, Scorpios have strong regenerative and adaptive skills. Knock 'em down, and they'll pop right back up again... and they'll be looking for vengeance. Just like their celestial arachnid representative, people born under the sign of Scorpio can be creepy, suspicious, and up to no good. They also change their minds about things—or people—lightning fast.

All this makes it sound like Scorpios are really terrible, but there are a few good things about them, too. Because they have such a fierce and passionate approach to life, they charge at obstacles like a battering ram. They're good pals to have, as long as you can keep on their good side. Seriously—whatever you do, don't cross a Scorpio or you could end up in huge trouble. They'll destroy any fool stupid enough to get in their way.

Scorpios want to know everything about everyone, and are not shy about asking. They want to know how you're feeling, what you're thinking, and what made you think that way. No question is too personal for a Scorpio, and they may even enjoy watching you squirm while you find a way to answer them without feeling completely and utterly *stripped naked*.

Speaking of being stripped naked, Scorpios enjoy stripping you both metaphorically and literally through methodical seduction. They are highly sexual people. However, what attracts so many people to Scorpions is not their heat... it's their ice-cold demeanor. They're the ultimate gamer when it comes to picking up on their love interests, and can apply the same hard-to-get style in business negotiations as well. If you find yourself unable to explain why you are so strangely motivated to please the Scorpios in your life—that's Scorpio's magnetism at work.

LOVE AND RELATIONSHIPS WITH SURLY SCORPIO

Let's just get it out of the way, why don't we? Scorpios are hot to trot. They're ready, aimed and loaded. They love their Vitamin F—and we don't mean fatty acids. They are the most sexually charged sign in the zodiac and they wear their sexuality like a badge of honor. Just because their libido is high, however, it doesn't mean that their standards are low. They may just stay home and practice by themselves until they find just the right sparring partner to take into the ring. When they find a romantic interest they fancy, very little can interrupt their pursuit. Scorpios have that tendency to seek out what they want and push societal standards and morality to the side.

Some plants and animals come encoded with natural warning signs. Red berries are poisonous, yellow insects can sting you, and scorpions are designed to communicate that they'd just as soon kill you as look at you. If a predator makes the mistake of getting too close to a scorpion, *boom*. The scorpion will engage that poisonous tail and kill, kill, *kill*. While Scorpio people don't have obvious physical traits that clue in potential love interests to their vicious moodiness and fiendish, ice-cold temper, their birth date alone should be enough to warn away the suitors. Unfortunately, it's usually not enough to put them off.

There is a reason that Scorpios keep ending up in long-term relationships when everyone knows they should be avoided like the plague... they are master manipulators. They can turn any negative into a positive, flip any script to make them seem like the misunderstood good guy. They are the spiders who invite hapless insects to their doom. If you find yourself in a Scorpio's web, make no mistake: they had this planned the whole time. Scorpios are calculating and careful—and detail oriented enough to make their goals into a reality. However, once you stop having sex long enough to make up the bed and take stock of your situation, you'll discover the hidden truth about your Scorpio. In the early days of the relationship, you thought the PDAs were a sign of how affectionate your lover was, but now you can understand that they're just a means of advertising to the world that you are his or her property. You once thought that the persistent questions about your day were intended to prove engagement, but now you see that this constant checking-up on you is actually a vicious jealousy rearing its nasty, Scorpion-shaped head.

CHECKLIST FOR DATING A SURLY SCORPIO

You'll need a least half of these things to have a successful relationship with a Surly Scorpio

Neckbrace: You'll spin your head faster than Linda Blair did in *The Exorcist* trying to keep up with a Scorpio's mood changes. Sometimes the change is logical but most of the time it's completely unpredictable and a bit of whiplash is unavoidable.

Time: Scorpios don't want your money, they want your time. Well, they may want your money as well, but the time is a definite. Scorpios need plenty of time to get to know you initially, they'll need loads of one-on-one romance time, and of course they'll then need an appropriate amount of time to take over every aspect of your entire life.

Eye contact: When Scorpios try to communicate with you earnestly and genuinely, watch their eyes. They can speak out of both sides of their mouth in order to get what they want, but their eyes don't lie.

Loquaciousness: Scorpios are rarely attracted to the strong, silent type—they need to be actively entertained by stimulating conversation. The Scorpio is a gatherer of facts by nature and is fascinated by the inner workings of the human brain. He or she will happily let you talk yourself right into a corner. Just remember, everything you say can and will be held against you in the Court of Love.

Bedside manner: Making a Scorpio angry is one of the four worst mistakes you can make in life. To avoid this detrimental mistake, you should develop an excellent bedside manner with your Scorpio. Learn how to deliver bad news with grace, and how to be respectful and kind when you communicate with your Scorpion. If you fail to master these things, prepare to be destroyed.

Good sportsmanship: Scorpios are highly competitive and they *do not like* to lose. Usually, they're also athletic, strong, and will probably beat you at any game you play together. Be a good loser, and life with your Scorpio will be easier. If you pout, they will use it against you in the worst possible way.

SURLY SCORPIO COMPATIBILITY

SCORPIO AND ARIES LOVE

You argue so often and with such passion that it's actually kind of a turn-on for you now. This couple really gets off on the roller-coaster effect of fighting and then making up. And as long as they can work things out in the bedroom, they should be able to get along fine... most of the time.

SCORPIO AND TAURUS LOVE

If you can combine Scorpio's desire for unadulterated power and Taurus's need to accumulate wealth and possessions, then you'll have a power-couple on your hands. These two will attack their careers as fiercely as they attack each other behind closed doors.

SCORPIO AND GEMINI LOVE

A Scorpio-Gemini combination would make a really good pair for a sting investigation. Gemini would talk off the mark's ear while Scorpio snooped around and got the facts. If they don't plan to open a private eye company, however, they will definitely run into trust issues. Gemini's a flirt, plain and simple. This, combined with Scorpio's fierce possessiveness, can only end in tears being shed.

SCORPIO AND CANCER LOVE

When a Scorpio and a Cancer get together, they create a beautiful, secure home that they both love. They enjoy spending time together in their home and taking on unwieldy projects with each other. The main problem with this match is that Scorpio will walk all over Cancer as if he or she were a damp bath mat.

SCORPIO AND LEO LOVE

Leo is completely ego-driven and Scorpios take a lot of pride in lowering the egos of those around them. Leo will switch back and forth between pouting and strutting, trying to fluff up his or her self-esteem, while Scorpio will apply him- or herself and work hard to invent new and exciting ways to knock Leo down a peg or two.

SCORPIO AND VIRGO LOVE

Virgo is a simple thing. He or she puts everything out onto the table. For Scorpio, the truth can only be accessed by flipping a hidden switch on the table, pulling down on a candlestick attached to the wall, swiveling a full-wall bookcase in the library, and creeping down a dank corridor to find the hidden safe. Which then has to be cracked. Virgo will never understand Scorpio's need for secrecy and privacy. Virgo will always feel like he or she is being manipulated.

SCORPIO AND LIBRA LOVE

There can be great romance between a Scorpio and a Libra. Both enjoy the art of seduction and the two can experiment without restraint on one another. Libra also balances out Scorpio's intensity and lightens up their mood. In this match, Libra brings a lot of positive emotions to the relationship. So, to make things fair, Scorpio should probably earn a lot of money or have other particularly redeeming qualities.

SCORPIO AND SCORPIO LOVE

The obsession that this match feels toward one another borders on the downright scary. They want to live each other's lives, breathe each other's air—and probably more! These two risk compromising one another's career and family relationships when they pair up, because there's simply not enough room for that much passion in a single person's life.

SCORPIO AND SAGITTARIUS LOVE

Sagittarius is playful and light, while Surly Scorpio walks around as though storm clouds are swarming

over his or her head. Scorpio will condemn Sagittarius's flighty attitude and try to tame him or her. Sagittarius will quickly tire of Scorpio's need to control everything and their natural reaction will be to pull back. This relationship will probably end up breaking down into a "Dear John," letter or text message... It's only a matter of who hits "send" first.

SCORPIO AND CAPRICORN LOVE

This is a solid match, although it's basically the greatest Axis of Evil of the zodiac. This couple will pursue power and money to no end and flatten anyone who gets in their way. This is the twosome that constantly name-drops and criticizes mutual friends at dinner parties, and then under-tips because one or both of them felt their server was slightly distracted during the appetizer course. They're the couple that argues against having a bake sale at the school because it distracts the kids from studying. They simply do not bring out the best in one another... or in humanity.

SCORPIO AND AQUARIUS LOVE

Scorpio is a thinker and Aquarius is a doer. Aquarius will bristle at Scorpio's incessant pondering and lack of focused action. If these two don't get on the same page early on, the relationship won't even get off the ground. And if they do make it, it's because the sex is really good—there's just no other explanation. Others may not envy your regular public arguments and drawn-out battles of the will, but everyone will be able to tell that something special goes on behind those closed doors.

SCORPIO AND PISCES LOVE

This couple is a successful one in the dating stage, but once kids and other responsibilities are added in... it's all over. Before the responsibilities, both could sort of pass by the difficult conversations and ignore the major differences. Pisces could daydream, Scorpio could plan and plot, but when this couple has to work together to figure out night feedings, preschool applications, and PTA meetings, real life will hit them hard and they will find that they're not on the same team after all.

CAREER AND MONEY FOR SURLY SCORPIO

Some people freeze in their tracks when a professional problem arises. Scorpios swoop in, quickly analyze the key issues, experiment with different tactics, and solve it. A Scorpio gets the job done. They will also happily train everyone on the techniques they used to troubleshoot it. It sounds great until about two weeks later, when they're still bragging on about how they solved that problem with such focus and determination, and knocking down their boss's door with requests for a promotion. Scorpio does not play it cool when it comes to discussing his or her madly brilliant skills.

Don't call them out on anything, though. If you tell a Scorpio that they're being obnoxious, they'll immediately begin plotting their revenge on you. It's not that their skin is particularly thin, but they hate criticism and will hold a grudge if they decide that you've been disrespectful to them. They will work long, tireless hours if they think that their team appreciates their efforts. If not, they will dig their heels in and become completely uncooperative.

Scorpios are social manipulators. They locate people's weaknesses and home in on what they can use to their own advantage. Because of this, they make excellent negotiators and analysts. They take a great deal of pride in a successful day at work, and pride is one of their primary motivators. Scorpios want to feel that swell of gratification and the self-satisfaction of a job well done. And they sure wouldn't mind it if everyone else patted them on the back, too.

ABSOLUTE WORST JOBS FOR A SURLY SCORPIO

Social worker: You know that scene in the movie where the social worker *really gets through* to the troubled teen and helps them to turn their life around? Yeah, that social worker is *not* a Scorpio. Scorpios simply don't empathize with others enough to be social workers, though they would probably enjoy some of the sordid stories that they'd hear in this line of work.

Public relations expert: While Scorpios have a great deal of swagger in person, it does not necessarily translate well to video. They may find their television-selves stumbling over words or just coming across as cold and harsh.

Servers: A Scorpio lowering themselves to wait on others? Never... But, err, never say never. Scorpios know that they'll have to work their way up in their careers and that they won't enjoy it. Oh, and they make terrible waiters. They know that Table Nine needs refills. They just don't *give* a damn.

JOBS THAT A SURLY SCORPIO MIGHT NOT SCREW UP

Forensic detective: Scorpio has a stomach and a constitution strong enough to get them through even the most visceral of crime scenes in order to figure out whodunnit. They'll ask all the right questions, dissect the body to find out exactly what happened, and they're naturally suspicious enough to chase down the guilty scofflaw. Note: this job may not actually exist outside of television shows, but if it does, a Scorpio would be shoo-in for it.

Collections Agent: Most signs would be nervous about picking up the 'phone to call up total strangers and demand money. Not Scorpions. They are confident in their mission, persistent enough to complete it, and forceful enough to get people to pay up. They are smart with money and can negotiate to find a solution that will appease them. Their empathy is mostly at the low end of the scale, so they don't even mind putting a single mom and nine kids out on the street. It's all in a day's work.

Dominatrix: Scorpios look great in leather. Their sexuality is a natural turn-on to most clients, and to those who need a little more pain with their pleasure, Scorpios also have the temperament to dominate their lovers and shame them into submission. They also have the dedication to act out other people's fantasies. It's *Fifty Shades of Scorpio*, and yes, please, may we have another?

STARS OF THE SIGN SURLY SCORPIO

When Scorpios have something to say and they find the right medium to express themselves, the world takes note. In the world of fine art, Scorpio painters have pioneered new techniques. Both Pablo Picasso and Claude Monet ventured outside of the popularly accepted styles of their day to create exciting and memorable works. Scorpio Georgia O'Keeffe broke the mold and explored her strong sexuality through her *double-entendre* flower paintings, and Bob Ross continued to push the envelope by finding new ways to render happy little trees.

On the silver screen, many of Hollywood's absolute hottest actors fall under the sign of the Scorpion. The following men are all fully fledged sex symbols and embody the sign's steaming magnetism: Leonardo DiCaprio (along with Kate Winslet, he added the *Titanic* to the list of most common settings for sexually fantasies... even though it's at the bottom on the ocean); Ryan Reynolds (*People Magazine*'s Sexiest Man of the Year 2010); Ryan Gosling (star of the "Hey, Girl" meme); Matthew McConaughey (hot in every movie, but especially the *Magic Mike*); and Owen Wilson (who is at his most attractive when he has his mouth closed and his shirt off). Scorpio ladies are well represented in

Hollywood as well. These women are classic beauties, but moreover they are intelligent and funny and simply enchanting. Actress-turned-princess Grace Kelly was a Scorpio, along with stunning and contemporary stars Anne Hathaway, Julia Roberts, and Rachel McAdams. Oh, and despite the sign's dead-serious reputation, the lovely comedienne Emma Stone proves that Scorpios can, in fact, have a sense of humor.

Another hilarious and sexy Scorpio works on both sides of the entertainment industry. Seth MacFarlane is creator of the so-wrong-it's-right animated sitcoms *Family Guy* and *American Dad*. MacFarlane is massively multitalented. He can act, sing, direct, and produce, injecting his vulgar and insulting humor into everything he does. In fact, since his work offends viewers universally, it's lucky that he has the aggressive and self-righteous Scorpio characteristics to power him through the critique and opposition. Other well-renowned directors—such as Ang Lee, Peter Jackson, and Martin Scorsese—were also born under the sign of Scorpio, proving that Scorpios who are given the influence they so desperately seek, along with a medium to effectively speak to the world, can effectively use their powers of emotional manipulation on millions of people. That's so Scorpio.

SURLY SCORPIO BIRTHDAYS

⚡ LIBRA–SCORPIO CUSP
People born between October 20 and October 25 were born into the Libra-Scorpio cusp and can display traits

of both signs. Since both Libra and Scorpio are known to change their minds, people born on the cusp can take this to the extreme. They can switch careers, hobbies, friends, all at the drop of a dime. People born in this cusp have the semi-unlucky curse and/or blessing of being simultaneously the sexiest and least loyal people in the entire zodiac... so just keep that in the back of your mind if you're considering making one a long-termer.

⚡ OCTOBER 23

October 23rd-ers keep the strangest things secret. They'll treat even the most socially acceptable love affairs like dirty little secrets, and make their lovers jump through hoops to keep the details of their encounters private. They also keep quiet about more mundane things, such as what they had for lunch, how many cups of coffee they drank, and where they hid the victims' bodies.

⚡ OCTOBER 24

On October 24, in 1901, sixty-three year-old daredevil pioneer Annie Edson Taylor was the first person ever to go over Niagara Falls in a barrel. Straight after being fished out of the river, she reportedly said, "No one ought ever do that again." People born on this date have to try for themselves to discover what they like and what they don't like—and they end up trying out lots of different things because they have a very hard time deciding what they want out of life.

⚡ OCTOBER 25

If you date someone born on October 25, he or she will never stop comparing you to their ex. They might have enough class not to say it out loud, but you should know that—subconsciously—everything you do is being measured against their first love. After your relationship gets really serious, you'll graduate and they'll begin comparing you to their mother or father, so that will be fun, too, eh?

⚡ OCTOBER 26

Most Scorpios don't gravitate toward public speaking, but two famous American politicians share this birthday: Theodore Roosevelt and contemporary leader Hillary Clinton. People born on this day are hungry for power and have very few close and trusted friends. They are thick-skinned and can withstand harsh criticism while passionately championing causes that matter to them. They've also been known to carry big sticks when the occasion called for it.

⚡ OCTOBER 27

When October 27th natives enter a new relationship, their love is the Sun and everything in their life revolves around it. They hide away from the rest of the world to completely immerse themselves in their infatuation, and their Universe shrinks to hold only their lover. Famous poets Dylan Thomas and Sylvia Plath both share this birthday and both lived in a world of love-fueled, manic depression. While Dylan Thomas essentially drank himself to death, Sylvia Plath put her head in the oven. If you were born on October 27, it's best to avoid poetry altogether.

⚡ OCTOBER 28

What is a good friend? An October 28th native may not be able to delineate the specifics and draw a

191

blueprint for you, but they will certainly let you know when you're *not* living up to their expectations. People born on this day have a strict set of standards for how they expect others to treat them, and when someone crosses the line, the trust is gone forever. These are people that will hold a grudge for years until it becomes a fully fledged feud.

⚡ OCTOBER 29

October 29th-ers expect the people in their lives to go to nearly impossible lengths to prove their love. They need to be constantly reminded that they're adored, and will feel betrayed if ever they don't feel adequately appreciated. Infamous Nazi propagandist Joseph Goebbels is an October 29th native, which just goes to show the extremes that someone born on this day will go to in order to take revenge on people who disrespected them—or just didn't love them enough.

⚡ OCTOBER 30

Enough with the third degree, October 30th-er. If you were born on this date, you *need to know.* You want all the facts, all the gossip, all the information you can get. Googling is very likely one of your favorite hobbies and you may even struggle at work or at school because you're constantly following up on trails of inquiry. You give your friends twenty questions and might turn off potential love matches by launching an inquisition into their deepest secrets during your first date.

⚡ OCTOBER 31

People born on October 31 make do. Each day they evaluate their resources and options and make decisions based on what they have to do. They will adjust their tactics at any point to better meet short-term goals. For example... Lorena Bobbitt, who was born on this date, woke up one morning and decided that her husband had one too many body parts, so she took matters into her own hands to solve the problem.

⚡ NOVEMBER 1
In their friendships, romantic relationships, and careers, November 1st natives must at all times feel as though they're important. They need to be a vital part of a project in order to give it their best. They need to feel as though they are in control of their households and a key player in their friendships. Basically, they're the star of the show and everyone else is a bit player. If a friend, lover, or colleague fails to make a November 1st Scorpio feel like the center of the Universe, they will simply disengage.

⚡ NOVEMBER 2
People born on November 2 have stamina. They have staying power to a degree rarely seen in humans, and not just in the bedroom—although the bedroom is a good place to witness it first hand if you're game. They are stubborn as well, and refuse to see the viewpoints of others even when confronted with logical arguments. Marie Antoinette, the famously spoiled and ill-fated Queen of France, was born on this day and took her refusals to compromise her own beliefs to an extreme, and hence paid the ultimate price.

⚡ NOVEMBER 3
The world is a harsh place, right November 3rd native? You frame everything you've ever done as a polarized situation you've had to single-handedly

overcome. Your education was achieved in spite of the teachers and school boards who conspired against you, and your love affairs were all illicit and frowned upon by members of authority. In your career you've had to rail against endless rolls of red-tape and argue down incompetent managers. It's always a story of you against the world, and anyone who tries to argue with that world view will simply become another obstacle you have to overcome.

⚡ NOVEMBER 4

If you've ever spoken to a friend or family member about something you're stressed out about, and they've said, "You should just *relax*," then you know the frustration of spending time with someone born on November 4. They have a hard time really *hearing* someone else's point of view and immediately write off everyone else's problems as trivial. The only way to get them to treat a problem seriously is to make it *their* problem, at which point they'll spring into the quick-and-decisive action of the Scorpio.

⚡ NOVEMBER 5

If your birthday falls on November 5, you enjoy burning people with your barbed, cutting sense of humor. Everyone laughs publicly at your jokes to be a good sport, but make no mistake—they almost always go home to cry into a pint of ice cream after a visit with you. On November 5, England celebrates Guy Fawkes night—a night for fireworks and bonfires. Just mind that your friends and family don't accidentally throw *you* on the fire instead of their effigies.

⚡ NOVEMBER 6

Family is important to people born on November 6. One of their primary goals in life is to create a stable family, and this goal is ever more important to them if they had a bad time growing up. For example, Bobby Beausoleil, born on November 6, thought he had found the perfect family as an adult—until he realized it was actually The Manson Family and got arrested for murder in 1969.

⚡ NOVEMBER 7

You simply cannot rush someone born on November 7. They refuse to be hurried along, shooed out the door, or complete anything hastily. This doesn't mean that they are always behind on a deadline or running late—they know themselves well and give themselves adequate time to complete their tasks. They move slowly and sometimes finish ahead of people who overbook and make themselves crazy. So, if you are a person who is always busy, rather than thinking of November 7th natives as simple-minded, lazy, and dawdling, you should probably think of them as the tortoise that's going to kick your quick little butt in the long run.

⚡ NOVEMBER 8

If you were born on November 8, your life view is a little... off. It's not always a bad thing, and many people who share this birthday have gone on to be very successful. Milton Bradley, famous game inventor and creator of *The Game of Life*, was born on this date, along with the author of the gothic novel *Dracula*, Bram Stoker. Hermann Rorschach, the man who invented the inkblot test to take a peek into the mysterious workings of his patients' minds through mostly phallic-looking blobs, was also born on November 8.

⚡ NOVEMBER 9

November 9th natives really want to find true love. They never stop looking—even after they're married and have a family. To help them in their noble search for a love to trump all other loves, they'll employ any means necessary. From accounts on online dating sites to speed dating to spending all night talking to people at the bar... they will go to the ends of the Earth to find the passion they seek. If you're currently dating or married to someone born on November 9, try to overlook the fact that they know with absolute certainty that something better is out there.

⚡ NOVEMBER 10

It's vital for people born on November 10 to get in touch with their spiritual beliefs at a fairly early age. If they do not settle on the idea that there's some sort of cosmic retribution for their earthly acts, they are likely to be absolutely abysmal human beings and hurt everyone around them over and over again. If unchecked, they'll essentially become gratification machines: ruthlessly competitive at work, overweight and overindulging on too much food and alcohol, and somewhere on the careless-cruel spectrum with their friends and family.

⚡ NOVEMBER 11

The American World War II novel *Catch-22* was published on this day in 1961. As the title indicates, the book follows a young soldier who is damned if he does, damned if he doesn't. People born on November 11 feel that this is their fate as well. They have a hard time understanding what matters and what doesn't in the long run, and so they try to do *everything*. They vacillate between extremes in an attempt to get their rudders straight, fasting or feasting in all areas of their life, which unfortunately leaves them with less satisfaction and less clarity than when they began.

⚡ NOVEMBER 12

November 12th natives are not the most popular kid on the playground. In fact, they seem to really polarize their friends and colleagues—people either champion them or despise them. Because of the dramatic feelings they incite in others, they tend to be socially independent and untrusting of others and do really stupid things to the people that they love. They feel the need to test the strengths of their few personal relationships over and over again, and in doing so they end up driving away the people who actually care about them.

⚡ NOVEMBER 13

People born on November 13 don't just want to avoid being on the bandwagon. They want to strip the bandwagon for parts and set it on fire. They work very hard to set themselves apart from others and establish their own unique tastes. While they might bring interesting new styles and sounds to the table, people born on this day may find themselves insulted when they realize that the only determining factor in a November 13th native *hating* something is the fact that other people *like* it.

⚡ NOVEMBER 14

Scorpios tend to ask a lot of questions and people born on November 14 elevate this trait to a fine art. November 14th-ers want to know *everything* about you, *everything* about your family, *everything* about your friends, and so on and so on. They will keep you talking until they squeeze out every little secret that they could use against you. The U.S. Republican Joseph McCarthy, famous for launching a communist witch hunt in the 1960s, was born on this date. His feeling of total entitlement to prize open the personal lives of citizens, and then persecute others with the unearthed details, is a prime example of how these Scorpions roll.

⚡ NOVEMBER 15

Once bitten, twice shy, right November 15th-er? If people on this date have ever been burned, they take their lessons to the extreme. If they were hurt in a love affair, they'll give up on finding true love and just settle for someone dependable. If a project blew up in their face at work, they'll go to great lengths to avoid making the same mistake again, even switching jobs if that's what they feel is necessary. Some might say that this makes them cowards, but people born on this date are confident in their knowledge of the world and how they want to interact with it.

⚡ NOVEMBER 16

On November 16, 1849, Russian writer Fyodor Dostoyevsky, author of *Crime and Punishment*, was sentenced to death for anti-government activities. He was led out in front of a firing squad, blindfolded, and then—at the very last moment—his execution was staid.

After doing time in a Siberian work camp, he returned to Russia and spent much of the rest of his life in debt and sorrow. November 16th-ers are able to see Dostoyevsky's life as a complete success, whereas others in the zodiac might think of this as unjust and cruel. All his pain and suffering *meant something* and represented ideas bigger than the actual facts. To someone born on November 16, transcending life to create a legacy of ideals is the noblest thing a person can do. Whether or not there's a happy ending involved is entirely beside the point.

⚡ NOVEMBER 17

People born on November 17 see the big picture. Their success in life comes from being able to channel and develop creative talents in other people. Lorne Michaels, producer of *Portlandia, 30 Rock,* and *Saturday Night Live* excels in this arena, as does prolific Hollywood director and producer Martin Scorsese, both of whom were born on November 17. The downside to looking at the big picture, however, is that people born on this date can focus so much on the wider view that they miss out on the little joys right in front of their faces.

⚡ NOVEMBER 18

There is a lot of judgment coming from your side of the room, November 18th native. Even if you hide your social adjudications with polite manners and constructive comments, you think everyone else is weaker than you, stupider than you, and less capable than you are. Even if someone beats you outright, you invent a thousand excuses for why you lost. You're not always wrong about your own abilities versus those of others, but in the end you're always the loser... because

199

being a bad loser and constantly arguing about why you're better than everyone else will make you very lonely very quickly.

⚡ NOVEMBER 19

Murderer Nathan Leopold was born on November 19. By all reports he was a genius and his nannies even said that he spoke his first words at four months old and had an off-the-charts IQ. As he got older and entered college he became completely obsessed with committing "the perfect crime." If you were born on November 19 and are reading this, you're probably narrowing your eyes and nodding your head slightly. You know this feeling of obsession with the idea that things can be completed flawlessly. You probably have your own plans to pursue some object to its perfection, whether it's loading the dishwasher with maximum space-efficiency, or running a perfect mile, or putting together the ideal outfit. Good luck to you in your pursuits, but please keep in mind the fact that Leopold's obsession ended quite *imperfectly* with him promptly getting caught after killing a teenager. So, there are no guarantees of satisfaction in this way of life.

⚡ NOVEMBER 20

November 20, agree or disagree: it is morally acceptable to not tell the whole truth sometimes. You probably said that you disagree, right? For some reason, people born on this date are all about the truth, even though it hurts the people they love. They can even negatively impact on their own career by firing up that truth cannon at the workplace. While telling the truth is always admirable, telling the boss that his ideas are totally unoriginal is never a good idea—even if it is true. And it probably is.

⚡ NOVEMBER 21

November 21st natives tend to be rather tight with their purse strings. They want to amass wealth and see spending as the opposite of wealth, rather than a part of it. Hetty Green, born on this day, is in the *Guinness Book of World Records* for being the stingiest woman alive. She was a millionaire who inherited riches from her father and invested them wisely. Nicknamed "The Witch of Wall Street," she's said to have worn the same dress for years and denied her family access to a doctor—much to their detriment—because of the cost. If you are a November 21st native, chances are you are not quite as extreme as Hetty Green, but if you find her an inspiration rather than a cautionary tale... ooh, that might be a red flag.

⚡ SCORPIO–SAGITTARIUS CUSP

If your birthday falls between November 19 and November 23, you are on the Scorpio-Sagittarius cusp and can display the characteristics of both signs. People born on this cusp have Scorpio's intensity mixed with Sagittarius's impulsiveness, which means that they pursue new ideas with the fervor of a dog chasing a tennis ball. They throw themselves headfirst into projects without always thinking through to the possible repercussions of their wild actions.

STINKING **SAGITTARIUS**

NOVEMBER 23 TO DECEMBER 21

*L*aissez les bonne temps roulez, Sagittarius. Life's a freaking party, and you're the guest of honor. If you were born under the sign of Sagittarius, congratulations, you've rolled lucky seven in the giant craps game that is life.

For anyone who has never had the pleasure of knowing a Sagittarius up close and personal, they're the type of people who give off a friendly, warm vibe twenty-four hours a day. It's disconcerting, like they're able to cast this spell and draw people into their tractor beam without even trying. Sagittarius is the new girl in school who moves to town, immediately usurps you as the teacher's pet, then makes out with your boyfriend, and invites all your friends to a movie marathon sleepover at her house. The Sagittarius invited you to the sleepover, too—Sagittarians always invite *everyone* to their parties—but you're too annoyed to go, so you stay home and bitterly bite through an entire bag of Peeps, alone, in front of the television instead. This may be hard to believe when you're brutally decapitating

203

marshmallow chicks, but you'll probably come around eventually and become besties with that Stinking Sagittarius.

One of the qualities that attracts everyone—except for the most bitter and cynical people out there—is the jolly Sagittarian sense of humor. Sagittarians are really, genuinely funny. Not always funny in a clownlike way, but they have the natural wit and timing to add a sparkle of fun to conversations. Sometimes they'll cross the line, however, and get fast and loose with their humor. This can really hurt thin-skinned friends. Sagittarians tend to hide their true emotions behind their jokes, which can give them a sort of sad-clown-Pagliacci-type-feel when they get down in the dumps. This makes for awkward social interactions and should be avoided.

Sagittarians are represented in the zodiac by the centaur—half-man, half-horse... strong, free, a good shot with a bow and arrow, and magnanimous by nature. While other signs in the zodiac torture themselves over right vs. wrong, good vs. bad, Sagittarii are generally immune to this sort of impotent self-sparring. They do put a lot of thought, however, into their place in the Universe and the role(s) that they should assume in their time on Earth. When they dream, they dream big, but luckily (and of course... they're *always* lucky) they have a little help from their friends. Rarely is there a story of a Sagittarius who truly pulled him- or herself up by his or her own bootstraps without the generous help of a friend or relative. Sagittarius may tell the story differently, but—deep down—they know they're mainly been carried on the shoulders of others.

LOVE AND ROMANCE WITH STINKING SAGITTARIUS

For some unknown reason, the Universe rewards Sagittarius for their minimal efforts at hard work with seemingly boundless luck. If you are currently dating a Sagittarius, *you* are a part of that luck. Chances are, they don't deserve you, but you just feel so inexplicably drawn to them. Don't waste too much time weighing up the inequities, because the relationship is bound to be over sooner rather than later. Sagittarius does not like being tied down in one relationship for very long, but—just like their Centaur animal guide—they prefer to leap freely through the wild wood, sowing their wild Centaur oats as broadly and widely as possible.

Sagittarians are incredibly physical, so if you're planning to keep one interested, bring on the sensuality. Try nightly massages, shoulder rubs, and big, warm hugs as often as possible. If you have to go on a business trip, it's best to buy your lover a puppy or a big, heated, human-shaped body pillow to fill the space you've left behind. Otherwise you might come home to find the mailman or pizza gal all over your pillow. Stand warned: if a Sagittarius cheats on you, it's really not their fault. It's *your own* fault for being way too boring. These Centaurs are incredibly high-maintenance partners. They need you to laugh at their jokes, even when they're only moderately funny. They need you to stimulate them intellectually and intimately while maintaining an air of highly sexualized mystery. And, of course, they need you to overlook the occasional clues of infidelity. If you're incapable of giving Sagittarius a long enough leash to hang themselves, they might just slip out of their collar and jump the fence.

While the cheating, the neediness, and the constant, awkward joke-making are all enough to make you super excited about getting hot and heavy with a Sagittarius, don't forget that they're also highly emotional creatures. When you talk about your relationship, you'll likely hear a diatribe—completely divorced from logic, by the way—about how they need a *huge* amount of independence, privacy, and time alone... because they're scared of commitment. Aw. Bless them. They might even cry. Tip: If you ever find yourself face-to-face with a crying Sagittarius, just tell them a dirty joke. The first one you can think of—the dirtier the better. Just distract them from their anguish long enough to wrap your arms around them. Once they're caught up in your warm embrace, they'll relax, and then you can properly comfort your sad Sag— or deliver the *coup de grâce* and walk proudly out the door before they can break up with *you*.

CHECKLIST FOR DATING A STINKING SAGITTARIUS

You will need at least half of these things to have a successful relationship with a Stinking Sagittarius.

206

Sense of humor: You have to be able to crack up with a Sagittarius. They are always joking around, so loosen up, don't get easily offended, and bust a rib at all their fart jokes, puns, and consistently inappropriate jokes. If you don't at least pretend like you have a sense of humor, Sagittarius will drop you faster than yo' mama dropped you on your head as a baby.

Stamina: A Sagittarius likes to be touched and physically stimulated constantly—as in, *all the time.* If you're not exactly a marathon runner in the bedroom, you better get into training because a five-minute hump session before firing up Netflix on your laptop will not keep a Sagittarian interested for very long.

Less than 20-20 vision: Having poor vision will help you to turn a blind eye to all the evidence that might ordinarily lead you to be suspicious of your Sagittarius. If you really want to stay together, just ignore the lipstick on the collar, or the middle-of-the-night texts. Just pretend you don't see it.

Patience: A Sagittarius might take a very, very, very long time to commit to you. They fall in love fast, but the idea of being with the same person for more than eight minutes can be pretty scary for them. Be patient. If you put pressure on them too early, they'll run away screaming.

Spirit of adventure: Be up for anything! A Sagittarius likes to get wild, and if you want to hang out with them, you'll have to go along for some crazy rides. Just shut your eyes tight, grab ahold, and try to have fun.

A little mystery: Look, you don't have to hold a dime between your knees or anything, but the longer you maintain some mystery between you and your Sagittarius, the longer they'll chase after you. The Centaur likes to zero in on his prey before he or she lets loose with their arrows of love, so just play it cool for as long as possible.

STINKING SAGITTARIUS COMPATIBILITY

SAGITTARIUS AND ARIES LOVE

Behind every great Aries is a great Sagittarius, or at least that's how Aries wants this relationship to be. Most of the time Sagittarius is happy to just pull the puppet strings. When it fails, it's usually because one or both parties loses interest in the other and strays outside the union.

SAGITTARIUS AND TAURUS LOVE

This will be the best two weeks of Taurus's life, and Sagittarius will very likely feel pretty damn blissed out as well. The physical explosion of chemistry that their affair sparks will be amazing. Knees won't stop shaking for weeks. However, unless Taurus really taps into their practically non-existant spontaneous and wild side, Sagittarius's fuse will burn out fast.

SAGITTARIUS AND GEMINI LOVE

Other than bickering about who should be on top, Sagittarius and Gemini get along. They're both super-social and full of energy and spontaneity. They keep up with each other—and with the Jones's. As a result, these two can really get into some deep debt if they don't find a good accountant.

SAGITTARIUS AND CANCER LOVE

In a lot of gangster movies, the gangster has a nice spouse at home—someone who cooks big, steaming pans of lasagna and raises their children—and then at least one or two well-kept lovers to keep life entertaining. Cancers could make really good mob spouses, especially if they don't go talk to the Feds when they find out that their Sagittarians are getting some side action.

SAGITTARIUS AND LEO LOVE

Sagittarius likes to laugh, and in a Sagittarius-Leo union, there will be plenty to laugh about. Mainly Leo's huge ego. Sagittarius needs to wear kid gloves when it comes to teasing Leo too much. A Lion with wounded pride could lash out, and things could get nasty pretty quickly.

SAGITTARIUS AND VIRGO LOVE

Virgo will never stop analyzing Sagittarius's unpredictable actions. Why did Sagittarius wear that outfit? Why did she use that inflection? Why did take that route to the airport? And more importantly, why did she go run off with that other guy? Virgo can analyze all day and never really understand what Sagittarius is thinking.

SAGITTARIUS AND LIBRA LOVE

These two will have an amazing relationship and a perfect life as they jet around the world, seeing foreign countries, visiting the Egyptian ruins and the Eiffel Tower and eating tapas in Spain and—oh, wait... they're not millionaires? Well then they'll spend their miserable little lives together, anxious, irritable, and constantly replaying the exact moment they went wrong.

SAGITTARIUS AND SCORPIO LOVE

So, when esteemed porno directors are casting, *this* is the match they go for. The Sagittarius and Scorpio match will physically lead to some incredible chemistry and experimentation that, if documented, could lead to cutting-edge breakthroughs for the entire sex industry. When they have their clothes on, they're much less likely to get along, however. Scorpio is just too intense for Sagittarius's light-hearted approach to problems.

SAGITTARIUS AND SAGITTARIUS LOVE

As long as they can find a qualified surgeon who will safely and affordably remove their respective feet from their respective mouths—as they both tend to speak before thinking about the other's feelings—then this might work. The primary problem for this match will occur way, way down the road when they're in their late thirties, when they have kids in elementary or middle school, and one day they just run out of jokes to tell each other. The silence that ensues will be *deafening*.

SAGITTARIUS AND CAPRICORN LOVE

Capricorn would have to get down from his or her high horse in order to date a free-flowing Sagittarius, and since that's not likely to happen, it's probably best to skip the whole affair. The two may be attracted to one another's exotic ways, but this will most probably be a very short-term attraction.

SAGITTARIUS AND AQUARIUS LOVE

Both Sagittarius and Aquarius are independent and need their space, and they're both really free thinkers. One of the big obstacles they'll face is that Sagittarius is much more focused on their own happiness, while Aquarius is determined to ease the world's suffering. Aquarius thinks Sagittarius is self-centered, and Sagittarius thinks Aquarius has a big soapbox shoved permanently up his or her—well, you know.

SAGITTARIUS AND PISCES LOVE

Pisces's mouth will be permanently agape as he or she watches the way Sagittarius interacts with the world. It's like watching a very rich person attempt to connect with a person who has lost everything, or, more accurately, never had anything at all. Pisces has spent his or her entire life feeling like a lesser member of society, while Sagittarius slides through life and somehow always lands on top. This dynamic can be stressful and may keep Pisces up all night worrying about the injustice of it all.

CAREER AND MONEY FOR STINKING SAGITTARIUS

Sagittarii are not the hardest workers in the zodiac, but they do have an incredible ability to see all the moving parts of a project and focus on what needs to be done at any given time. They are able to visualize their own successes naturally, without even taking the time to create a collage-style vision board. This ability for totally optimistic, big-picture thinking is one of the characteristics that helps to propel Sagittarius through changes, unscathed by the painful growing pains that plague the rest of the zodiac through life's transitions. And while this style of thinking can ensure projects get carefully executed, it also means that Sagittarius is always thinking about the next step. This can cause him or her to focus on the future instead of being present in day-to-day tasks.

Just like a Sagittarius will routinely get bored and fall out of love with paramours, they also need to be mentally stimulated—constantly—in the workplace or else their professionalism will drop off fast, like an anvil off a cliff. But not everyone can have the fascinating and highly varied jobs that would be best-suited for Sagittarius (see the list below). A boss managing a Sagittarius in a very dull job would do well to consider him- or herself a grown-up preschool teacher, and devise new and fun ways to get Sagittarius to maintain productivity. For example, if the position required a lot of 'phone calls, Sagittarius could try out different accents to see which one got the best reaction. Or if the position required a repetitive action, try speeding up or slowing down the assembly line randomly to keep Sagittarius on his or her toes. Reward stickers and recess periods help, too!

Most Sagittarii make terrific colleagues. They are natural storytellers, so their water cooler gossip is always really exciting. They usually have a lot of great personal stories to throw in about a near-death experience while rock climbing on Sunday, or the very dangerous guy they met on Wednesday night. They leave their colleagues inspired to forego book club and bingo for more exciting, free-time experiences. Sagittarians laugh easily in the workplace, take things lightly, and are unlikely to get swept up in the political dramas that can plague office environments.

ABSOLUTE WORST JOBS FOR A STINKING SAGITTARIUS

The boss: A Sagittarius should probably never, ever be the boss. Of course there are exceptions, such as if a particularly creative and ambitious Sagittarius starts a skateboard company or develops an app. Generally speaking, however, they change their minds too often, they're too generous and will give everyone unearned bonuses (including vendors), and they will be incapable of firing people for poor performance. If a Sagittarius finds him- or herself in the position of being the boss, it might be good to hire them an advisor from a more decisive and controlling part of the zodiac.

Navy Seal or other highly-trained professional military person: Centaurs are armed with a bow and arrow, and they make decent hunters and adore athletic competitions, but a Sagittarius is not the guy or gal that you want out in the field trying to ensnare a terrorist cell. Their focus can wane, they think everything is funny, and their drive is questionable at best.

Pharmacist or chemist: Sagittarians aren't exactly detail people, and they're not always a shining star when it comes to academic performance. These are not the best people to go to for accurate information about bad drug interactions, or to trust to properly cook up your methamphetamine. That said, they'd make excellent drug dealers or pharmaceutical reps, so they don't have to stay out of the biz completely.

JOBS THAT A STINKING SAGITTARIUS MIGHT NOT SCREW UP

Importer/exporter: Like Art Vandelay in *Seinfeld*, Sagitarii would make excellent importer/exporters. They could import long matches and potato chips, and export diapers—or whatever—but a job that combines travel with meeting new people and making money is a perfect match for a Sagittarius.

Foreign missionary: A job as a foreign missionary combines the excitement of travel, the independent spirit of being a trailblazer, and the natural communication prowess of a Sagittarius. Just add faith and a genuine belief in manifest destiny, and you're all set to head out on the adventure of a lifetime!

Doggie daycare owner: This is actually the best possible job for a Sagittarius. Aw! If every day a Sagittarius could get up and hang out with adorable pets and their people, they would have a very happy life. Sagittarius won't even mind picking up the poop, as they are eternal optimists.

STARS OF THE SIGN STINKING SAGITTARIUS

An inordinate amount of teen idol pop stars are Sagittarians. Miley Cyrus, Britney Spears, Nicki Minaj, and Christina Aguilera are all under the sign of the Centaur. These young women embody the Sagittarius spirit, with their high energy, sex appeal, and creative spirit—oh, and the total lack of self control to filter anything they say or do in public. They bounce from sordid love affair to sordid love affair, never slowing down to become burdened by a long-term commitment. Also, they all clearly have good managers who can help them to focus their energy for long enough to record an album. Sagittarius men are also drawn to strut their stuff on stage and in showbiz. In fact, famous guitar player Keith Richards, notoriously hot actor Brad Pitt, and wonder-director Steven Spielberg were all born on the exact same *day* under the Sagittarius sign.

Centaurs can find great success with the written word. Several famous poets, including Emily Dickinson, William Blake, and John Milton, are Sagittarii. Because of their teeny-tiny attention span, Sagittarius writers sometimes do better as poets than longer-form fiction writers, although a few have squeaked by as novelists. Do the names Mark Twain and Jane Austen ring a bell? How about C.S. Lewis and Louisa May Alcott? All Sagittarians. Once in a while, however, the creative gifts of the Sagittarius go a little wrong and then you get the dark-side writers such as the doomsday prophet Nostradamus or the conservative cuckoo Ann Coulter.

STINKING SAGITTARIUS BIRTHDAYS

⚡ SCORPIO–SAGITTARIUS CUSP

If you were born between November 19 and November 22, you were born on the Scorpio-Sagittarius cusp. You've inherited some of the traits from each sign, such as Scorpio's resolve to stick with things until they are complete, and Sagittarius's lack of real and tangible life goals. This combination basically means you'll keep banging your head against the wall with no idea of what you really want to accomplish... and since you don't have any true goals, you won't be able to stop. It's just a lifetime of aimless energy expenditure ahead of you. Don't worry, your lighthearted Centaur side and super-sexy Scorpio side will conspire to ensure that you have lots of fun along the way.

⚡ NOVEMBER 22

How much do you want to bet that November 22nd natives have a gambling problem? Put everything on black and roll the dice, because if you were born on this day, the odds are very high that you should avoid the casino, the office pools, that poker night, going to horse races, and even those flutters of fantasy football.

⚡ NOVEMBER 23

People born on November 22 fall harder and faster in love than most of their Centaur kin. They get their feelings hurt when their relationships don't work out, and spend a lot of time sulking and explaining to people why they'll never find true love. The truth is, they will experience more true love in their lifetime than most people do, so they should try not to linger on the sense of rejection they feel all too keenly.

⚡ NOVEMBER 24

November 24th natives want to pursue their own desires with total independence. The rules *be damned*, family *be damned*. If you were born on this day, you will follow your dreams and steamroll whomever gets in your way. Dale Carnegie, author of *How to Win Friends and Influence People*, was born on this day. So was serial killer Ted Bundy, who had a totally different approach to getting what he wanted from others.

⚡ NOVEMBER 25

Joe DiMaggio, one of baseball's all-time greatest players and the adoring second husband of Marilyn Monroe, was born on this day. November 25th natives dream big, very big, though most of them don't have the perseverance to turn their dreams into a reality. If they do, they may realize, just like Joe did—eventually—that living the dream isn't always all it's cracked up to be.

⚡ NOVEMBER 26

November 26th-er, there's your way... and there's the highway... and there's not a whole lotta room in between. People need to get with your life view in order to have a successful partnership or relationship with you. To complicate matters further, you don't have any real idea exactly where your way is leading. That's OK. As Lewis Carroll famously wrote in *Alice in Wonderland*—published on this day in 1865—(a line that George Harrison famously paraphrased in his last single, *Any Road*), "If you don't know where you are going, any road will take you there."

⚡ NOVEMBER 27

People born on November 27 are very independent and love being the center of attention. Famous badasses Bruce Lee and Jimi Hendrix share this birthday, though it's important to note that they both died young through unnatural, strange, and somewhat mysterious circumstances. So, there's an upside and a downside to your stubbornness. On the upside, you'll probably be forceful and persuasive enough to get exactly what you want out of life. On the downside, you might die suddenly... and relatively soon.

⚡ NOVEMBER 28

Nearly 500 years ago, Portuguese navigator Ferdinand Magellan sailed through what was to be known as the Strait of Magellan for the very first time. Those were different times, when the physical world was still being discovered and mapped. If you were born on November 28, you crave that feeling of fresh discovery and often direct it inward, trying to map your feelings and understand the cause and effect of your own psyche. Try reading classic literature for insights—in many ways literature already exists as both map and mirror to our own psyche. Hashtag deep thoughts, hashtag *Bad Birthdays*, hashtag it's all been done already.

⚡ NOVEMBER 29

A few years ago, an electrician came forward on this date and revealed that he had over two-hundred-fifty original Picassos. The guy said that Pablo Picasso just *gave* him the paintings before he died, more than thirty years ago. So, out of thin air, a huge amount of work by a famous artist just *appears* one day. You have hidden paintings, too—or rather, you have valuable, unique, and precious parts of you that are currently buried. They are buried because they are really pretty dark, and you are scared of what others will think if and when you materialize them. Let it go, and start experimenting to find the right medium for expressing your inner self.

⚡ NOVEMBER 30

You're... hmmm, how to put this delicately... If you were born on November 30, you're kind of a dick. Too rude? Sorry if it hurts your feelings, but most likely you've said worse to people already today. And it's early in the day. You're like the morality police for everyone else, but when it comes to your own actions, there's always some excuse about why you have to behave how you do. Famous dicks born on this day include: Mark *"In the first place, God made idiots. That was for practice..."* Twain, Winston *"My tastes are simple: I am easily satisfied with the best..."* Churchill, and Billy *"I love it when someone insults me. That means that I don't have to be nice anymore"* Idol. Dick Clark was born on this day as well, and by all public accounts, he was a great guy—but he was married three times, so... maybe his ex-wives know something we don't.

⚡ DECEMBER 1

December 1st natives are usually smart enough to get by, and pretty damn funny to boot. Unfortunately, they think that's all they need in life to get by, and they neglect the give-and-take it requires to form real connections with friends and family. This can be a real curse, and often leaves the December 1st-er feeling lonely and aimless, even when they're surrounded by others. Woody Allen, Sarah Silverman, and Richard Pryor were all born on this day, and they're all able to channel their humor and social dissatisfaction into decent comedy.

⚡ DECEMBER 2

On December 2, 1942, University of Chicago scientist Enrico Fermi executed the first ever nuclear chain reaction. Which, of course, continued on as a global political chain reaction after the atomic bomb was developed and dropped, and which now continues on as a social chain reaction as nations try to understand the inequities that lead to warfare. And on it goes. Sagittarii born on December 2 see life as a chain reaction of sorts. They understand the interconnectivity of events, and how each aspect of their lives is like a falling domino, triggering the next. This can be empowering if they can control the direction of the dominos, but very depressing if they can't stop the dominos from tumbling long enough to change course.

⚡ DECEMBER 3

You didn't have it so good when you were growing up, right December 3rd native? Even if you were not financially struggling, you were starved emotionally or not nurtured enough. People born on this day feel like their deprived youths give them license to be over-competitive, and downright mean sometimes. They veil their nastiness with humor, but when they cross the line they can really alienate those around them. Their core is deeply unsatisfied and they will spend their entire life subtly trying to bring others down to their level.

⚡ DECEMBER 4

December 4th residents are typically really in touch with their inner spirit, or at least they spend a whole lot of money trying to get in touch with it. They will try green tea enemas, week-long fasts, sweat lodges—the whole bit. Sometimes it works, sometimes it doesn't. They make intense connections with people and ideas and drop them just as quickly, without letting themselves linger on guilt or responsibility. They need a job that they can take with them, a freelance or contract gig that allows them to be flexible—while they don't mind not having luxury items, they do need some way to fund their crystal healing and magnet therapy habits.

⚡ DECEMBER 5

If you were born on December 5, you're like a perpetual child. In a good way, not in an unfortunate Michael Jackson or Peter Pan way. You've found a way to preserve the magic and awe of childhood and channel it into meaningful, adult activities. Walt Disney is a famous Sagittarius born on this day, and his legacy and kingdom should be a symbol to December 5th natives, a reminder that they never need to grow old—and they certainly never need to *die* when they can simply cryogenically freeze their bodies to be revived in the future.

⚡ DECEMBER 6

People really like you, and you really like people, December 6ther. There are probably three or four people who call you a best friend, which, while it completely cannibalizes the meaning of the word *best*, is a testament to your good nature. This good nature makes you really easy-going—maybe *too* easy-going, as you are willing to give up your dreams the second that achieving them seems too difficult or stressful.

⚡ DECEMBER 7

On this day in 1972, the *Apollo 17* spacecraft took off into space. After clearing the Earth's atmosphere, the astronauts took a photograph known as "The Blue Marble," and sent it back down to the people on Earth. In the photograph, a blue sphere sits on a black background, swirls of white clouds gathering around the southern part of Africa and the Indian Ocean. It is breathtaking. No one decides they want to be an astronaut for the money. Instead, they do all the training, all the studying for that one moment—that opportunity to see Earth from way up above, a child's plaything in an infinite play yard. Like an astronaut, you are not particularly motivated by money. You pursue your goals for some singular moment. It may come once a day, once a month, or once in a career.

⚡ DECEMBER 8

People born on December 8 dabble quite a bit in this and that, but the second that something gets hard or slightly depressing, they're *out of it* like a shot. They know about a lot of things, but unfortunately they only know just enough to get themselves in trouble. So, if you were born on this day, try to keep deep and lengthy discussions about topics to a minimum. Tips for bullshitting: a) Listen a lot and speak only when you know you can add something useful; b) Don't get sucked into arguments with people. You can say something like, "It's interesting you feel that way," without losing face; c) Parcel your little bit of knowledge out carefully, inserting your opinions as filler. Follow these tips, December 8th-er, and live a long and prosperous life without ever really having to learn much about anything.

DECEMBER 9

Groucho Marx once famously said, "I refuse to join any club that would have me as a member." Sadly, people born on December 9 don't have the luxury of being so flippant about their membership in groups—in fact, their group membership is the whole basis of their identity. They're Sierra Club members, or Presbyterians, or alumni of Georgetown or *whatever*. They use the people they've associated with as a substitute for who they really are.

DECEMBER 10

The entire world celebrates a very special birthday on December 10. The first ever issue of *Playboy Magazine* was sold, stuffed into a plain brown paper bag, and rushed home for careful examination on December 10, 1953. Unlike the red-hot magazine that shares this birthday, people born on December 10 are cool customers. They simply walk away from friendships or relationships that cause anxiety. They handle stress at the office with confidence and calm. They can be very difficult to date (or parent, for that matter) for this reason, because not even the biggest guilt trip can make them stumble.

⚡ DECEMBER 11

December 11th natives won't settle for anything less than a fairy tale romance. They meet someone they're interested in and immediately cast themselves as prince or princess, and encourage their lover to act the part of the other. When real life butts in to dissolve the fantasy, they become heartsick and angry. While many Centaurs have a strong sense of self-confidence, December 11th-ers tend to feel slighted and undeserving of true love or true happiness. Therapy can help only so much—unfortunate events are written in the cards for people born on this day.

⚡ DECEMBER 12

Frank Sinatra was born on December 12, 1915, and as a young adult the crooner ran around with a group of other performers nicknamed the Rat Pack. Humphrey Bogart, Dean Martin, Sammy Davis, Jr., Peter Lawford, and Joey Bishop bopped across Vegas and California with Sinatra and Co., all having a swell time. Friends are everything to people born on December 12, and well after his death, Sinatra is still known for the tight bonds of friendship he formed with others. The downside to being so wrapped up in your friendships is that you're a sucker for peer pressure. If you buddy up with people who abuse drugs, alcohol, or Cheetos, you are likely to live a sickly sort of lifestyle. Try to find better friends.

⚡ DECEMBER 13

Unless they actually have diagnosed OCD, which is not fun at all, people born on December 13 can make their quirky, superstitious behavior really enjoyable! They might do things like cross the street if they see a black cat, or say people's names backwards to remember them, or some other creepy, quirky things that they keep secret for fear of being judged. And they do fear being judged, which is one of the reasons they keep their family and social visits to a controlled minimum. If they see people only one at a time, and don't linger for too long, no one will gang up on them—or so they hope.

⚡ DECEMBER 14

There's something fishy about people born on December 14. While many young adults in this day and age are desperately trying to differentiate themselves from their peers and exploit what is unique about them (usually via witty Facebook posts or animated gifs), people born on December 14 actually pride themselves on being fairly typical. Their childhood was OK, save for some rebellious years as a late adolescent. They made some good friends after high school and they have a nice routine. Secretly, though, way down deep... they desperately want someone with cultural authority to come up to them and say, "You're a very special little monkey. I can see through the totally mundane act to the brilliant star that's underneath."

⚡ DECEMBER 15

You're totally happy-go-lucky, right December 15th native? You're the typical Sagittarius, just friendly and happy and popular and—whoa! Wait. Why are your knuckles white as you're reading this? That vein in your neck is sticking out again. Quick, deep breath—smile and act cool. Give a little chuckle and roll your eyes. It's no big deal, right? It's just a bad birthday horoscope. The truth is that you're very dark and intense and you take things very personally—you're kind of an emotional monster, or at least a dreary sad-sack, hiding behind all the good times and laughter. It's obvious that you don't think it's funny and are a little weirded out as you read this. Don't worry. Your secret is safe here.

⚡ DECEMBER 16

People born on December 16 tend to get what they want out of life. Sometimes that's a good thing, and they can structure their life around making a living and raising a nice family, and other times it's not so good. Friends and family may try to intervene without realizing that a less successful December 16th-er has actually *chosen*, through conscious choice, the pathetic life they're living.

⚡ DECEMBER 17

Orville and Wilbur Wright were just two country boys from North Carolina, but their aircraft control inventions changed the history of aviation. Their first successful flight, a ten-minute journey, took off and landed on December 17, 1903. This flight was a culmination of years of toil, tinkering with simple machines and studying and getting to know the mechanics of moving parts. People born on December 17 need to spend a long time gathering information before they take action if they want their ideas to soar. If they don't do their homework, their careers are likely to crash and burn.

⚡ DECEMBER 18

December 18th natives are more likely to brag about the number of hotdogs they ate in one sitting than the fact that they received their law degree from Harvard. They are boastful and excited about things that the rest of the world sees as completely trivial, and prefer to keep the details of their professional successes and failures a secret. They love to help others and hate to ask others for anything, which makes them a really good one-sided friend to have, especially if they're also super-rich like guitarist Keith Richards, actor Brad Pitt, and director Steven Spielberg, who were all born on this day.

⚡ DECEMBER 19

Every conversation with someone born on December 19 begins the same way. "I just think I need to keep at this." Depending on what they're working on, they might actually be right—although it could seem weird at the time. These people have tunnel vision and they also try to bring everyone they know into their vision, either eliciting emotional support or actual, practical assistance on projects. Some friends might feel turned off by the confluence of social and professional life, but unless you are a trash collector or a manure spreader, most pals will be happy to collaborate.

⚡ DECEMBER 20

December 20th natives can kind of turn the super-friendly Sagittarius spirit into something slightly stalky and creepy. They will seek out people they admire and try to form friendships. Part of it is so that they can show off a little bit and say, "Oh, so-and-so? Yeah, we're friends (online)." But, primarily, the reason they do this is to study the friend and try to absorb—via osmosis or transference—whatever it is that makes them so successful. They really want to dissect and emulate the traits they appreciate in others, which can be both flattering and slightly threatening.

⚡ DECEMBER 21

Everyone's a hack. Half of the stuff that's out there physically disgusts December 21st natives. They just don't understand why people that don't have unique intellectual insights would put their ideas out there. After a party or other social gathering, it takes a December 21st-er at least a couple of hours to get the bad taste of *poseur* out of his or her system before engaging in a normal conversation again. They tend to be fairly considerate in person, and would rarely come out and accuse someone of being artless (though it's likely that a majority of hater-esque YouTube comments are made by people born on this day).

⚡ SAGITTARIUS–CAPRICORN CUSP

If you were born between December 19 and December 22, you fall into the Sagittarius-Capricorn gap. Your Sagittarius tendencies give you a good bedside manner, unlike most Capricorns, and because of this you can get far professionally. You think of life as a jigsaw puzzle, and when you decide to have a romance or expand your family, you slot those other people into your existing framework without even attempting to adjust who you are to fit your new responsibilities. This stinks for the people who are 'slotted in', but you're charming enough to make it worth their while.

CURSED CAPRICORN

DECEMBER 22 TO JANUARY 20

You don't suffer fools, Capricorn. You don't waste your time trying to protect people's feelings with trivial efforts such as "being nice" and "having manners." Manners are platitudes better left to the feeble-minded or lazy. And you think pretty much everyone is either feeble-minded or lazy—usually both. Incompetence is a plague on this land.

Try to relax, Capricorn. Take a breath and turn the tight little corners of your mouth upward into a smile. You come off like an incredibly frigid fish when people first meet you and it is hard to get through your armor to know the *real* you. When your inner circle does get to see the real you, they're in for a treat: they'll get to see the over-sensitive, over-reactive, suspicious, jaded side of you. They'll also get to know your pervasive pessimism, general grumblings, and your quick temper.

Those closest to you also get to know your insane workaholic side. You don't care how long it takes to get the job done right... you're going to stay at the office and figure it out. You'll miss dinner, and if the work's still not done, you'll just go in at dawn to finish it off. You wear blinders when you're trying to achieve a goal, and not much can slow you down. Other people can gum up the works when they constantly seek your advice. You'd like to refuse, but you have a strange and stubbornly charitable streak. More importantly, you tend to be insecure and *really* don't want to be seen as Scrooge-like. You know that most people already think you're a wet blanket. Unfortunately, no matter how charitable you are with your advice, you aren't likely to change their minds. Damned if you do, damned if you don't. Hell is other people, eh, Capricorn? Capricorn, the Sea Goat, will always be the zodiac's antagonist.

LOVE AND RELATIONSHIPS WITH CURSED CAPRICORN

First things's first. Are you absolutely, positively sure that you want to date a Capricorn? They're known for being critical, moody, angry, judgmental, and—worst of all—completely snooze-inducing. But, if you are punishing yourself for something you did in a past life or have another sadistic reason for dating a Capricorn, there are a few things you should know before diving in.

If you're in the unlucky position of being romantically linked to a Capricorn, it's probable that he or she found you, chose to pursue you, and won your heart through sheer hard work and perseverance. This wasn't a snap decision that you were "the one"—oh no, far from it. Instead, much like a serial killer stalks and sizes up his prey, your Capricorn studied you from afar to judge you from head to toe before deciding that you might make a good romantic partner. When the time was right, *POOF*, there was Capricorn everywhere you looked, wearing you down until you finally agreed to a date. Or got a restraining order.

If, on the other hand, the Capricorn was the hunted, your early dates likely consisted of a series of awkward conversations and uncomfortable silences. In the Capricorn's mind, these were all trials he or she devised to determine your relationship-worthiness. If you're still dating, condolences—you passed the Capricorn's tests. It is a testament to your assets, as Capricorns would prefer to feel desperately lonely and sorry for themselves (as they often do) than to settle for anyone that didn't pass muster.

How do you know for sure if a Capricorn is into you? Oh, look, his right eyebrow is slightly raised. He *loves* you! She wore a high-necked dress instead of a business suit. She's head over heels! Their signs of infatuation are subtle, for sure, but be on the lookout for uncharacteristic warmth and a lack of biting, sarcastic comments. In fact, your Capricorn leaving the office for your date is a pretty significant sign that they dig you.

Once you're in a relationship with a Capricorn, you'll start to realize that their organization and ambition are really useful to have around. You will enjoy great perks such as alphabetized bookshelves and a color-coded linen closet. If you get really close to a Capricorn, in the inner-circle, you'll even get to hear some of his or her jokes. If you pretend to laugh, it will go a long way toward sealing the deal. On that note, Capricorns are usually eager to seal the deal and might propose before you can say, "I prefer a princess-cut."

CHECKLIST FOR DATING A CURSED CAPRICORN

You'll need at least half of these things in order to have a successful relationship with a Capricorn.

Decorum: *Do not*, repeat, *do not* go out on a date with a Capricorn looking disheveled, or with your cleavage hanging out in an effort to be sexy. Don't get nervous and drink too much and get sloppy. If you keep yourself together, and make believe you're not the disgusting human you actually are, you might get a second date.

A plan: You need a plan for the evening. Not just where and when—it's also important to plan what you're going to talk about. You might want to make a ready-reference list of ten or so conversation topics that prove you're intelligent. Work in a few jokes for bonus points, and for double bonus points have back-up plans and emergency back-up plans. Note: the "plan" is different from the "long-term plan" (see below).

A long-term plan: Not only do you need to be able to talk to your Capricorn about what you want to be doing five minutes from now and five hours from now, but also what you want to be doing in five days, five weeks, five months, five years, five decades, and even longer than that. He or she needs to know that you have at least considered what it might be like to spend the rest of your lives together.

Adventurous spirit: Ordinarily, Capricorns are incredibly boring. But they do find weird hobbies to throw their additional energy into. They focus on these hobbies, sometimes to the exclusion of all else. So, even if you're not into fly-fishing, or hiking, or taxidermy, unleash your adventurous side and be willing to give anything a go.

The ability to keep your mouth shut: Capricorns ordinarily are not interested in what Jane said to John, or what Chris said to Cathy, or how many gummy bears you ate yesterday, no matter how impressive the number might be.

Wit: If you're naturally witty, you'll be in good shape. If you're not naturally clever, study up on some puns to work into conversation. Capricorns like puns more than other astrological signs, though they'd never admit as much in polite conversation.

CURSED CAPRICORN COMPATIBILITY

CAPRICORN AND ARIES LOVE

Aries will drive Capricorn into an early grave, and that's not just an expression. Capricorn will worry so much about all the impetuous things that Aries does—and his or her stubborn refusal to plan ahead, all the risks Aries takes, plus all the money Aries spends—that

Capricorn's heart will simply stop. Aries is really the winner in this scenario, as Capricorn will leave Aries all the money he or she has accumulated.

CAPRICORN AND TAURUS LOVE

This match is one of the most boring in the zodiac. Capricorn probably works late, while Taurus cuts coupons. When they go out to dinner it's because Taurus found them a great GroupOn deal, but it's never fun because Capricorn always thinks the service stinks, or the food's not up to par, or the decor is tacky. Once a year Taurus helps Capricorn to unwind with birthday sex, and they check that off their to-do list.

CAPRICORN AND GEMINI LOVE

This match works if you think of Gemini as Genie and Capricorn as Major Nelson. When invited out of the bottle, Gemini will try everything in his or her power to make Capricorn happy... but will simply manage to screw everything up. Capricorn will have to clean up the mess, and will send Genie back to the bottle. Any other power structure will make both parties miserable.

CAPRICORN AND CANCER LOVE

This match works tolerably well. Cancer helps to make a home for Capricorn, and Capricorn helps to awaken Cancer's ambition. Capricorn can calm Cancer down when he or she throws a tantrum, like a tough-love parent, and vice versa. Cancer can also help to spice up Capricorn's dull day-to-day existence.

CAPRICORN AND LEO LOVE

Both of these signs like nice, material things. They like to look good, they like to spend money, and they like to *make* money. They like music and travel. They should probably never breed unless they can afford to hire a great live-in nanny to raise their children—between all their travels and shopping, and the work that pays for it all, they'll never be at home.

CAPRICORN AND VIRGO LOVE

When *Virgo* is the relaxed one in the relationship, it's a red flag that the romance might be less than rewarding. As far as the work ethic goes, these two bring out the best in each other. They could make a great professional partnership, but their bedroom life consists mostly of them correcting one another on the best ways to achieve orgasm. "You might want to try a more circular fashion," or, "I believe a modified position might be best for someone of your torso length," *et cetera*.

CAPRICORN AND LIBRA LOVE

Capricorn appreciates romance, and Libra's full of it. Full of it, indeed. Libra's also full of gossip, compliments, optimism, and impracticality. Capricorn can smash all of Libra's hopes and dreams in mere seconds if he or she unleashes his cranky, critical side. This relationship works much better as a friends-with-benefits or booty-call situation, rather than as a long-term partnership.

CAPRICORN AND SCORPIO LOVE

This relationship is a very slow starter. Even if there's attraction when the two first meet, they will circle around one another like dogs looking for a place to go to the bathroom before finally giving in to their more primal urges. As these two signs mature and get to know each other better, their relationship will strengthen into mutual respect.

CAPRICORN AND
SAGITTARIUS LOVE

To a Sagittarius, dating a Capricorn feels a little bit like going out with your high school geometry teacher or your friend's married dad. There are pros to the situation: the Cap will always pay for the date and they make the Sag feel exciting and sexy... but Sagittarius may also feel like he or she is not really respected as an equal.

CAPRICORN AND
CAPRICORN LOVE

What makes the Debbie Downer skits from *Saturday Night Live* really funny is that sad Debbie is surrounded by upbeat, optimistic people who really want to make the best of the situation. Two Capricorns in a relationship together are a little like two Debbie Downers—but with no optimistic spoil to help lighten the mood. It's a real bummer and should never happen.

CAPRICORN AND AQUARIUS LOVE

Capricorn has no idea where Aquarius is coming from. To a Capricorn, trying to understand an Aquarian's logic is like trying to talk to a horse. Capricorn wants to get the bridle and bit and tame the wild Aquarius, but Aquarius fights and bucks the whole way. Whether they'll be able to gallop off together into the sunset is anyone's guess, but hopefully they'll put the riding crop to good use while they're trying to make it work.

CAPRICORN AND PISCES LOVE

Pisces is super-hot for Capricorn's intelligence and stability, but to Capricorn a Pisces seems like an eternal child. The Pisces is just so sensitive when it comes to Capricorn's criticism, and Capricorn will quickly get their fill of tears, tantrums, and melodrama. This couple's fights will begin to echo those of a teenager and parent during the throes of a hormone-driven, adolescent rebellion.

CAREER AND MONEY FOR CURSED CAPRICORN

The force is strong with this one... and by force we mean bloodthirsty ambition. Capricorns zero in on their professional targets and work obsessively until they meet their goals. These are classic workaholics, and have a way of tuning everything else out except their object. Whether they are trash collectors or CEOs, Capricorns are completely driven to succeed in their tasks. The only reason to not hire a Capricorn is that they are *too* hungry for success and might steal your job the first chance they get. Their ambition usually trumps any warm, fuzzy feelings of fairness.

A Capricorn is that guy in the office who puts everyone else to shame. If there are ever contests to build morale or incentivize sales, this guy will win it without even trying because he works *that* much harder than everyone else. He makes it more annoying by making it look like he's barely lifting a finger, and always goes above and beyond the brief just for fun. He or she's got a "system" and a "plan" and when asked about it, just shrugs, and says some humble-brag like, "Hey, it might not be the best plan, but all I know is that it works for *me*." Capricorn is also a snappy dresser and looks stylish all the time. Comparatively, colleagues usually look like they just got off the train from Frumptown (if the train was delayed and the on-board bathroom was out of order). This makes the Sea Goat's easy professional victories all the more irritating.

Most of the time, Capricorns get along with others in the workplace, primarily because they're good at what they do and they're organized. It's unlikely that a Capricorn has ever been awarded a congeniality award, so don't expect a lot of chit-chat when you're teaming up with a Sea Goat. They're not going to care what you thought about the final episode of *Breaking Bad*, or what Donna from accounting was wearing today. They will judge you mercilessly while soaking up all the relevant information that they can use against you—or others—in the future. They don't even mean to be completely evil, but sometimes that's the end result of mixing judgment and ambition.

ABSOLUTE WORST JOBS FOR A CURSED CAPRICORN

Social media manager: In no way is a Capricorn suitable for a job that would require them to be social, care about and share the latest gossip, or "Like" stupid things that other people post online. They refuse to lower themselves to the least common denominator in order to join the conversations that plague the globe's social media channels.

Relationship counselor: Capricorns do not want to sit there while you hash out what your sister said to your mother about your ex. When faced with other peoples' social problems, Capricorn's baseline response is a clear, resounding, "*NOPE... not getting involved.*"

Stay-at-home parent: Some signs make very nice, warm, fuzzy parents. Capricorns care capable of tolerating their own children, but their skill set is better suited to the professional sector than the home front. Three-year-olds need hugs, not bullet points. Capricorns might also find themselves disappointed with their children's slow development and, if overly involved in child rearing, they'll quickly become *those* parents. You know, the ones that yell at their kids after baseball practice or look disappointed at a second-place trophy from the science fair.

JOBS THAT A CURSED CAPRICORN MIGHT NOT SCREW UP

Web code developer: Many zodiac signs would run screaming if asked to sit at a computer desk and stare at their monitor for hours, working on one single line of code. For a Capricorn, that's the best day ever. They are detail-oriented and really enjoy blocking out the rest of the world to solve the problem in front of them. They may require a pizza break at 11pm, but they'll stay on it until the job's done.

Financial planner: Trust your money with a Capricorn. They will make it grow. Not for your sake, but for their own satisfaction in a job well done. The Sea Goat is clever when it comes to finding out-of-the-box solutions to problems. They retain information, they're good with numbers, and they will be able to find good investments for you within your comfort zone. Capricorn will, of course, want a sizeable commission for their hard work. They're not running a charity.

Non-profit organizer: If a Capricorn *does* run a charity, he or she can be very successful in meeting the group's goals. Whether they're raising money for radioactive fish in the Pacific or helping to instill shame in mothers who use formula instead of breast milk, Capricorn will get the job done through careful planning, wise delegation, and tireless execution.

STARS OF THE SIGN CURSED CAPRICORN

Oh, Capricorn, when you go big, you go *big*. Like Psy, the Korean genius behind *Gangnam Style*, the hip-hop song that took the world by storm in the summer of 2012. Without his Capricorn focus and dedication, Psy would never have been able to memorize and perfectly execute all his complicated dance moves. Elvis Presley is another world-famous musician that falls under the sign of the Goat. In fact, many very talented Capricorns have made it to the top of the music industry due to their extreme concentration and their tolerance for repetitive practice—these include Ellie Goulding, Dolly Parton, Janis Joplin, and David Bowie.

The intense Capricorn work ethic shows up in other fields as well. For example, the Duchess of Cambridge Kate Middleton displayed the same tenacity while she carefully worked her way into Prince William's heart and straight into Buckingham Palace. First Lady Michelle Obama is also a Capricorn. Most Capricorns are too buttoned-up to show off their humorous side to the world, but when they do, the crowd loves it. Comedian Andy Kaufman was a Capricorn, and so are Jim Carrey, Steve Harvey, Seth Meyers, and Dave Attell.

Many of the strangest authors are also Capricorns. Their work ethic allows them to focus and write prolifically. Their obsession with and dedication to their work ensures that the worlds they create are flawless and seamless. Capricorn J.R.R. Tolkien, for example, created an alternate reality in Middle-Earth and Stephanie Meyer hypnotized the world with her tales of vampires in the *Twilight* series. Famously cranky author J.D. Salinger perhaps best embodies the Capricorn, with his reputation for being a smug pain in the ass.

CURSED CAPRICORN BIRTHDAYS

⚡ SAGITTARIUS–CAPRICORN CUSP
If you were born between December 19 and December 23, you fall on the Sagittarius-Capricorn cusp. This means you display some of the most egregious traits of both signs, like Sagittarius's impulsiveness and Capricorn's full-on ambition. The combination of which means that you often make

business decisions that hurt others and that you end up regretting. Both signs have an independent streak, which means people born on this cusp hate working for "The Man."

⚡ DECEMBER 22

December 22nd natives feel shy in large groups, but because they have the traditional Sea Goat Capricorn swagger, they come off as snobby or rude. Or at least that's what they *want* people to think. The truth is, they're actually just snobby and rude but use their shy act as justification for their bad behavior.

⚡ DECEMBER 23

In 1888, on December 23, Vincent van Gogh sliced off part of his earlobe with a razor blade while in the throes of depression. People born on December 23 sometimes feel like they, a bit like van Gogh's earlobe, are unmoored. It's as if those born on this date feel that they were once attached, but then quickly—and without warning—became *detatched*. They might blame many things for causing this disconnectedness, but it feels permanent and irreversible, and a little bit dark.

⚡ DECEMBER 24

Let's face it, no matter what religion you are, it stinks to be born on Christmas Eve. Your birthday is always overshadowed by your friends' and family's anticipatory greed toward their own holiday bounty. You would never admit to this, but even as an adult you're still bitter about it. You hate yourself for being so needy, but you just want something that's all about *you*; something that you don't have to share.

⚡ DECEMBER 25

You are obviously in good company sharing a birthday with Jesus Christ. However, what no one really talks about is the fact that if Christ had lived past thirty-three years of age, He would probably have gained weight and developed health problems as a result. That's a tendency of people born on December 25. Truthfully, the ability to multiply fish and wine probably wouldn't have helped Him to keep His weight under control in the long run.

⚡ DECEMBER 26

If you were born on December 26, it's highly likely that at least once or twice since you began working you took a vacation. You had high hopes for this vacation to ease some of your stress-related headaches and backaches, but while you were on vacation, instead of relaxing, you found new things to worry about. If you were on a cruise, you couldn't sleep for worrying that the boat might sink. If you were at the beach, you thought about hurricanes and tsunamis. It's just not in your cards to ever *really* relax.

⚡ DECEMBER 27

Yes, you're demanding. December 27th natives set a very high bar for perfection, for themselves and for others. They can be unrelenting as they encourage others to higher and higher performance. But, hey, Louis Pasteur was born on this day, and just *think* of what might have happened to the world if he hadn't been a total hard-ass and developed the pasteurization process. If anyone ever questions your inability to compromise on quality, now you have total justification. Give them the old one-two Louis treatment.

⚡ DECEMBER 28

On this day, December 28, more than 400 years ago, Galileo was the first man to identify the planet Neptune through the telescope that he himself had fashioned (copying those already created in western Europe). Twenty years later he was found guilty of suggesting that the Earth revolved around the Sun, and eventually placed under house arrest until he died. Like the Roman Catholic Church, December 28th natives do not like change. They rail against revolution and will go to great lengths to keep things at the *status quo*, even if it means refusing to recognize the truth.

⚡ DECEMBER 29

Capricorns have lots of integrity, and strive to follow through on all their goals. In relationships, December 29th-ers have a hard time keeping up their incorruptibility. They don't mean to stray from the plan, but just somehow end up—over and over again—in relationships that are the *opposite* of what they say they want. If you are in a relationship with someone born on December 29, you were definitely not your Capricorn's original vision of a perfect mate. Sorry.

⚡ DECEMBER 30

On December 30, 1924, Edwin Hubble looked into his prized telescope and saw—for the first time ever—other galaxies. In an instant, humanity's realm of existence expanded in all directions. If you were born on December 30... simply put, you are not crazy about this change. You'd prefer to keep your blinders focused on other possibilities, and just cruise through your productive, socially satisfying life without pondering the deeper questions of origin and existentialism. You're not the shiniest star in the Milky Way.

⚡ DECEMBER 31

It's all about you, December 31st-er, or at least that's what you're hoping. You are the king of the humble-brag, the queen of attention-stealing moves, the prince of deft conversational back-to-me moves. You think you're much more interesting than you actually are, and no one bothers to correct you because your efforts at staying in the spotlight are so desperate and amusing!

⚡ JANUARY 1

If you were born on January 1, you are a moral beacon to those around you. Except no one seems to be paying any attention to you. Wait, seriously, why isn't anyone publicly praising your efforts or scrambling to follow in your footsteps? You should probably talk louder when you condemn everyone else's behavior, just to make sure they hear you.

⚡ JANUARY 2

Like your Sea Goat brethren, January 2nd-ers have the potential to make a lot of money in their careers. If you were born on this day, you focus on your work and continually bust your hump to make sure you bring home the bacon. Unfortunately, you also can't resist the opportunity to make a quick buck and might even gamble it all on a magic bean.

⚡ JANUARY 3

You're a lone wolf, a cowboy, a ramblin' man (or woman). You don't need anyone—others will just slow you down. You're also a puppet master and able to get people to do your bidding. You're basically like the Wicked Witch of the West, except without the winged monkeys. You should get some winged monkeys.

⚡ JANUARY 4

Stress makes you look gross. If you were born on January 4, you get all blotchy and disgusting when you worry about things too much. The more you try to force yourself into relaxing, so that you'll look more attractive, the more uptight you get. It's like a truly icky, vicious cycle.

⚡ JANUARY 5

What is taking so long? To January 5th natives, everyone else seems completely incompetent. If only scientists could clone *you* and put you to work on all the world's problems, you'd have the place whipped into shape in no time. It's lonely being the only competent one in the world, isn't it?

⚡ JANUARY 6

If you were born on January 6, do you ever scratch your head curiously when people mention their "besties"? Do you ever wonder why the "Best Friend Necklace" exists? How could two people enjoy one another's company enough to want two halves of a broken piece of jewelry? Even though January 6th-ers have a group of associates and colleagues, these Capricorns are unlikely to ever connect with someone closely enough to want to own a busted half-necklace.

⚡ JANUARY 7

The Leaning Tower of Pisa made its fame and fortune *because* of its imperfections. Sadly, on January 7, 1990, the tower was closed to the public due to its instability... but for generations prior to its closing, people loved that tower primarily because it was half-cocked. January 7th native, you are like the Leaning Tower of Pisa, and instead of scurrying to fix all of your imperfections, you should simply accept that you are and always will be a deeply, deeply flawed human being.

⚡ JANUARY 8

A creepy number of very, very famous musicians share the January 8th birthday. Elvis Presley, R. Kelly, David Bowie... All are also highly sexualized figures. Elvis had his scandalous hip gyrations, David Bowie patented his own androgynous brand of lust, and R. Kelly is proud of his proclivity for giving golden showers... the moral is that people with a January 8th birthday are super-freaky, super-obsessive about their work, and super-creative. If they can balance these three superpowers, they can make it to the big time.

⚡ JANUARY 9

As a rough estimate, January 9th-ers spend eighty to eighty-five percent of their time in deep, inner conversations with themselves. They scold themselves for things they've done wrong, bully themselves into making changes (which rarely stick), and analyze the origin of their imperfections *ad nauseam*. They spend a lot of time thinking about their childhood and have often uttered the phrase, "I just wasn't prepared for the *real world*," or some such condemnation of their parents and schooling. Though they'll feel foolish and berate themselves for needing affirmations, January 9th Capricorns would benefit from signs hung around the house and office that read, "I'm good enough," "People like me," and "I'm not a narcissist. Repeat. I'm not a narcissist."

⚡ JANUARY 10

Working their way up from the mailroom sounds like a January 10th native's idea of Hell. They fume when their talent is not fully recognized, and seethe if they are not rewarded with regular, timely promotions. They are confident that they can out-think and out-manage the upper management, and are not shy about telling everyone they know. While ordinarily this would get someone in trouble, sometimes their forthright nature—plus their strange, swaggery sexuality—accelerates them up the ladder. Truthfully, though, their management skills are strong. So they only have to sleep their way to the top about half of the time.

⚡ JANUARY 11

On January 11, 1908, the Grand Canyon was opened to the public by Theodore Roosevelt. Since its opening, around 685 people have perished in the breathtaking scenery, many through committing suicide. January 11th natives can be like the Grand Canyon. They are strikingly good-looking, and they attract many friends and admirers. They inspire thoughtful, deep conversations and are considered to be a remarkable asset. There's something inside, though, digging into them a little bit at a time, and if others aren't careful to respect this Capricorn's most treacherous inner parts, it can lead to emotional horrors and heartbreaks.

⚡ JANUARY 12

If only you were a little bit taller... a baller. If you had a girl who looked good, you would call her. People who were born on January 12 feel like they never have enough, and never *are* enough. They come across as shy or stand-offish, and are constantly taking inventory of what the Jones's have, both materially and in terms of their emotional status. Are people happier than they are? Wealthier? More physically fit? Smarter? They have a tough time cheering on their loved ones if they think that someone's succeeding more than they are in any aspect of life, and can't help themselves from critiquing others' creative works out of jealousy.

⚡ JANUARY 13

People born on January 13 come across like loose cannons. While they could have inner restraint, they seem to others like frivolous, scattered, impulsive people. January 13th natives include that guy who sits around at a party in the suburbs talking about the time he was a stowaway on a cruise ship, but instead of getting into trouble he made friends with the captain and got to steer the ship. The gal who used to be a burlesque dancer before she decided to produce documentaries was probably born on January 13th. The worst part about them, at least to others, is that their impulsive decisions seem to pay off. It doesn't seem fair to be wild *and* find financial stability.

⚡ JANUARY 14

Romantic relationships with January 14th natives are almost impossible. They have competing desires: the need to control the home front and the relationship, *and* the need for secrecy and privacy. Together, this creates a powder-keg situation where their romantic partner can never be truly independent *or* truly a teammate. Unfortunately, January 14th-ers really need another half to help them to relax and control their anxiety. Without a lover, they will develop unhealthy habits such as eating every meal from drive-thru joints, or drinking too much to help them go to sleep. If they can't keep a romantic partner interested, they should probably live with their parents, or hire a night nurse or a live-in housekeeper, to give them some sort of grounding in society.

⚡ JANUARY 15

People born on January 15 have a big problem. They need to leave a mark on the world. The thought of becoming worm food before they create a legacy for themselves keeps them up at night. They are very hard-working, and once they figure out how they're going to make themselves immortal, they will work tirelessly toward achieving it. The pie in the sky is, of course, Martin Luther King, Jr., who shares this birthday. He has a whole day—a federal holiday—named after him! That's every January 15th-er's dream come true, but he's set the bar pretty high. Most people born on this day would be happier if they made peace with the fact that the best legacy they'll leave is a warning to all their children and friends not to worry so much about leaving a legacy.

⚡ JANUARY 16

Breaking with the usual Capricorn practicality, January 16th natives have a lot of *feelings*. Primarily, they are acutely aware of the inner-connectivity between society, nature, animals, and the earth. They like to trace the cycle of everything they do, following the lineage of their food from the seed to the farm to the store, from the store to the table to the bathroom to the ocean. This can get annoying in romantic relationships, because their bedroom waxing about boobies being the source of food for newborns, and our bodies being just bones covered with skin, and all pleasure being fleeting, and dust turning to dust, etc., can get a little dark and become a turn-off. Some people are into that, though.

⚡ JANUARY 17

Benjamin Franklin is among the many famously ambitious people born on January 17. Franklin's career is awe-inspiring and his trajectory from rags to riches is the foundation of the American Dream. He was beloved both in the United States and in Europe, and his legacy is one of innovation and technological advancement. But he was kind of a dirty dog in his personal life, never settling down and marrying, engaging in multiple affairs and wrecking homes on both sides of the Atlantic. For January 17th natives, it's difficult to "settle" romantically for a less-than-perfect match, and you hold your love interests to inhuman standards. You see an imperfect spouse as an anchor that would hold you back from reaching your full potential. If you do settle down and have a family, you will always look at them with a degree of resentment, even though you try to hide it for their sake.

⚡ JANUARY 18

Most people lie about the number of people they've slept with, because of social pressures. The common wisdom is to divide the publicized number in two for males, and multiply it by two for females, to get to the truth of the matter. January 18th natives are indubitably honest, so the number of people they say they've slept with is probably more-or-less accurate. And it's also probably pretty damn high. People born on this day are ruthless charmers, and they see notches on their bedpost as achievements. They also— most probably—keep a little black book because they genuinely like most of the people they end up with, and might even pursue professional relationships with their paramours after a little bumping and grinding with them. They have an extensive network and use it to both build their careers and meet new sexual playmates.

⚡ JANUARY 19

On January 19th, 1915, the first neon tubes were approved for advertising signs. Since that date, the world has seen many neon signs, some classier than others, hanging outside all sorts of establishments. If January 19th natives had a neon sign it would read in all its eye-scorching glory, "Open 24/7" but, of course, neon signs don't last forever. They tend to burn out after about 5,000 hours (208 1/3 days). People born on this day are exceptional friends. They genuinely love the people in their lives, but when their relationships hit the rocks, they just burn out completely.

⚡ CAPRICORN—AQUARIUS CUSP

If you were born between January 19 and January 23, you fall into the Capricorn-Aquarius Cusp. You have the competitiveness of the Capricorn and the sociability and passion of the Aquarius. It is vital that people born on the cusp participate in some sort of competitive game or sport, or they will find trivial little ways to beat down their family and friends until no one remains and they are all alone in the world.

AWFUL AQUARIUS

JANUARY 21 TO FEBRUARY 18

I f a load of people jumped off a bridge, Aquarius would stand on the edge of that bridge, looking down, wondering why people are so dumb. To the Water Bearer (Aquarius's zodiac representative), other people just seem like sheep following along with what everyone else is doing most of the time, hopping on bandwagons, getting with the latest craze, going with the flow. Where's the *originality*? Where's the individual thought? Aquarius proudly stands out from the crowd, a jet-black sheep amongst a sea of dusty, white wool. It's near impossible to fit Aquarius into any sort of mold and it's useless to encourage them to do anything they don't want to do.

Because of your Arian refusal to conform, you might have been the victim of some serious bullying as an adolescent, by less progressive peers, and as an adult you may find it difficult to shake off the feelings of being an outcast. Rest assured that you will laugh last in the end, when you're living the dream, working for

255

an environmental company up in Alaska, sleeping in a shack with spotty heat, or getting paid the big bucks to be a court-appointed social worker.

Water Bearer, you consider yourself to be quite the intellectual, and you get wisdom and inspiration from all different walks of life. For example, you might take as much insight away from a five-minute conversation with a philosophical junkie on a street corner than a full-semester college course. Granted, your parents might not be thrilled with your creative use of their tuition money, and less-than-excited to hear about your budding friendship with the wise old drug addict. Best not to tell them.

Aquarius, you have this certain, boundless energy that can really, acutely *bug* the people around you. It's not fair to you, especially because you have other peoples' well-being in mind at all times, though that doesn't change the fact that it's astoundingly annoying to be around you. You can be outspoken, judgmental, self-righteous, and unrelenting. You also use unnecessarily big-vocabulary words. You give brutally honest feedback instead of comfortable little white lies. When you're interacting with other people about issues that you care about, you come on with about as much subtlety as a Mack truck. Honest, truthful, and clear is the way of the Aquarius. And to be honest, a lot of people wish Aquarius would just get out of the way.

LOVE AND RELATIONSHIPS WITH AWFUL AQUARIUS

The Aquari people will not be smothered. If you have your eyes on an Aquarius and you're a clingy, together-all-the-time kind of person, you will certainly need to dial back your expectations of what it will be like to have an Aquarius as your life partner. While most Aquarians, like humans in general, enjoy being touched and sexually stimulated, they may prefer to keep separate bedrooms or even separate households for a long period of time. The perfect relationship for an Aquarius is basically an exclusive, friends-with-benefits type arrangement. If their partner refuses to agree to a booty-call-based lifestyle, Aquarius may agree, but they'll always resent their partner in the same way that a wild animal taken out of the jungle would resent their captors.

Some other astrological signs are born with a clue about which gender they'll want to date, and as these non-Aquarians grow into adolescence, it's quite clear that they either do, or do not, like yiff animations or furry sex, bondage, crazy sex toys, *phalloorchoalgolagnia*, *et cetera*. Aquarius, on the other hand, feels the need to experiment and to know first-hand what they like and what they don't like. They have a "don't knock it 'til you've tried it" attitude. Though the Water Bearer's sexual tastes may run a wide gamut, they are almost universally opposed to the sexual subjugation and abuse of people in the porno industry, so if you don't want to hear a long-winded speech on justice for all, it might be best to keep that vid suggestion under your cap.

Aquarians like to argue—they really enjoy it. They will debate everything, with you as their willing or unwilling sparring partner, from the type of peanut butter you purchased to the state of the government to the value of formal education. The best tactic to take with an Aquarian lover is to assume the role of an acquiescent adult with a child. Give them lots of choices, try to make them smile by doing fun things, and be a good friend—even when their behavior is so bad that what they really deserve is a spanking and to be sent off to bed with no dinner.

CHECKLIST FOR DATING AN AWFUL AQUARIUS

You'll need at least half of these things to have a successful romantic relationship with an Awful Aquarius.

A room: As in "get a room." Your Aquarius does *not* subscribe to PDAs. They don't think it's sexy to make out in the corner or get handsy under the table at dinner. If there's not an appropriate place to hook up, they are fine with skipping it entirely.

Confidence: The Water Bearer is not big on platitudes. You will not find him or her heaping compliments on you just to make you feel good or otherwise prop up your ego. They don't *withhold* compliments or anything like that, they just genuinely don't notice your new hairstyle.

Opinions: An Aquarius will not be satisfied in a love affair where they are the only one bringing strong opinions to the table. Since the Aquari people love to debate so much, you'll need to provide some of the material for those debates... or else Aquarius will simply choose something to argue about at random and take you off guard.

Household equality: If you end up living with an Aquarius, don't try to make him or her your pet or servant. Get your own drinks, cook dinners at least half of the time, load the dishwasher, and enthusiastically support his or her career. Otherwise, Aquarius will rebel against the feelings of constraint and household matters will be very bumpy indeed.

Patience: You'll need patience as Aquarius fills you in on their last ten lovers, patience when they get on their morality soapbox, and patience as they decide to appear distant and assert their independence. If you're really in it to win it with an Aquarius, you'll take it slow and not try to push any aspect of the relationship forward too quickly.

Fun: Aquarius can be decidedly un-fun (unless they're in large groups of friends, which seems to bring out their party-animal side). They need some glee injected into their lives, so plan adventurous dates, check out new restaurants, and definitely try that new sexual position you read about online.

AWFUL AQUARIUS COMPATIBILITY

AQUARIUS AND ARIES LOVE

It's hard to know what to expect from this couple. If you're outside the relationship, you'll feel your head spinning at all the spontaneous decisions that this couple makes. They might blow off family events to go rock climbing, or might decide to take a week-long ski rescue course together. They fuel each other's unpredictability and, while it drives their friends and family crazy, they have a pretty good time together.

AQUARIUS AND TAURUS LOVE

Dear Awful Aquarius, you've probably been told this multiple times in the past, but hear it now and absorb it once and for all: *Taurus does not like change.* You can't rearrange all the furniture to get a better flow while he or she is at work. Don't change your vacation plans at the last minute to surprise your Taurus mate. A Taurus will never feel really, genuinely comfortable with an unpredictable Aquarius mate, and may develop allergic hives as a result.

AQUARIUS AND GEMINI LOVE

These two will talk *a lot*. In their endless conversations about all things intellectual, Aquarius will debate,

Gemini will explore and ponder. The two of them will probably break out their smartphones or Google random references very often. They both just have a craving to *know* about the world, and this is a compatible match. Unfortunately, they might not make it very well in financial terms as both are impulsive spenders.

AQUARIUS AND CANCER LOVE

Cancer feels awkward when out with Aquarius's friends. As a result, he or she might drink too much or hide in the corner all night, texting. Aquarius thinks that Cancer is being stand-offish, or pouting, but really it's just incredibly uncomfortable for the Crab. Arguing also makes Cancer feel unsettled, and Aquarius often seeks out arguments. This match will be a painful one for Cancer, and Aquarius will find him- or herself in the role of the "bad guy" more often than is pleasant.

AQUARIUS AND LEO LOVE

If Leo and Aquarius get together, sometimes Aquarius will find him- or herself completely horrified with the things that come out of Leo's mouth. The ego and bravado is just such a turn-off for an Aquarius. Leo also strives for a lavish lifestyle and likes materialistic comforts, while Aquarius is more austere and less hung-up on possessions.

AQUARIUS AND VIRGO LOVE

Virgo is basically the rain on Aquarius's parade in this match. Aquarius has ideas, arguments, and plans to make the world a better place—but with a single swipe of logic and realism, Virgo can bring the whole fantasy crashing down. While Virgo may make good legal counsel for an Aquarian, they probably won't make good lovers.

AQUARIUS AND LIBRA LOVE

Both Aquarius and Libra really love people. They care about those less fortunate than themselves and may work together to bring about social change. The downside is... they both really love people and might have a hard time being faithful to one another. Since both signs have jealous and possessive streaks, infidelity could end an otherwise beautiful union.

AQUARIUS AND SCORPIO LOVE

Scorpio considers it a challenge to get an Aquarius, and once they set their mind on sealing the deal, not much can halt their pursuit. Aquarius will initially be attracted to Scorpio's magnetism, but will soon realize that a long-term relationship with a Scorpio means a lifetime of battling for control and independence. It might not be worth it.

AQUARIUS AND SAGITTARIUS LOVE

This combination is a fun match, with both parties bringing energy and ideas to the table. The Centaurs, however, tend to be far more shallow than the Water Bearers, and this will likely cause some mutual resentment. Aquarius just wants Sagittarius to genuinely *care* about the plight of the anglerfish, while Sagittarius just wants Aquarius to have a good time.

AQUARIUS AND CAPRICORN LOVE

Both of these signs abhor the idea of going along with the crowd for lack of individuality. Together, they will not try to keep up with the Jones's, not feel the need to get the latest kitchen appliance or watch the same television shows that the rest of the world is watching. They will probably clash when Capricorn rationally argues down all of Aquarius's new and exciting ideas. Aquarius will resent Capricorn like a grounded teenager and will do something to rebel.

AQUARIUS AND AQUARIUS LOVE

The problem with this combination is that there's nothing that really binds these two together. It's like trying to make a cake with flour and sugar. Both partners are detached, and neither feels a strong bond to their home. They will have fun together, but it's probably not in their best interest to reproduce or get an especially needy pet together.

AQUARIUS AND PISCES LOVE

There will be loads of projects that are started and never finished in this household. If you are in an Aquarius-Pisces relationship, look around. You'll probably see cans of paint stacked in a closet, maybe a ladder propped against a wall somewhere, and Post-it notes full of ideas stuck to everything. This couple will argue, frequently, about Aquarius's lack of affection and the Piscean's neediness, but if they can overcome these things, they may be able to tolerate one another for a long time... and they may even get around to finishing some of those projects.

CAREER AND MONEY FOR AWFUL AQUARIUS

Aquarians are "ideas people." Their ideal working day would consist of a few hours developing their brilliant ideas and a few hours talking about those ideas in a meeting. They will make sure that their voice is heard in one way or another, regardless of their rung on the corporate ladder. Aquarians usually have pet causes that they'll champion around the office, such as switching to recycled cups, or setting up a coat drive or a ride-share program. They gravitate toward working full-time for charities that support noble causes, but they will find some way to do good even if they're working for world's greediest, most polluting corporation.

An Aquarius who gets hung up on red tape can become incredibly frustrated. If you are planning on hiring an Aquarius, you might need to change your management style. Basically, you have to let them do whatever they want and just blindly hope that it raises the bottom line. Don't be surprised if you find a Water Bearer taking on the tasks of other departments—they hate silos in the workplace and prefer everything to be a joint effort toward a shared goal. Don't make an Aquarian do any evil or morally despicable tasks, either. They will never stop lecturing you on how terrible it is to plow the rainforest, or how wrong it is to make violent cartoons for kids, or how serious a crime tax evasion is.

An Aquarius needs a physical environment that they find pleasing in order to concentrate and be happy. To get more productivity out of the Aquarians on your payroll, consider repainting the place with nice, soothing colors and adding some decorative art. They will also bring in some personal style and pizazz to the office, and err toward very shiny and bold clothing choices, so a strict dress code is a major negative for an Aquarius.

ABSOLUTE WORST JOBS FOR AN AWFUL AQUARIUS

Veal slaughterhouse worker: If the mass slaughter of sweet little baby cows isn't enough of a turn-off for an Aquarius, the repetitive nature of slaughterhouse work might really frustrate him or her. An Aquarius really despises mechanical, non-thinking work, and hacking a rib rack off a cow's carcass, which is vilely swinging from a hook, will quickly get old and boring for an Aquarius.

Priest: To hear of an injustice through a sacred confession, and not become outraged—and not act on that outrage—would be too much for Aquarius to bear. They couldn't simply guide a confessor to ask for forgiveness. Instead, they'd probably turn into a vigilante priest and sneak out into the city at night to single-handedly right all the wrongs they heard about that day.

Hostage negotiator: Aquarians are notorious for their support of the underdog. They'd immediately arrive on a crime scene and feel bad for the criminals instead of the hostages. They might even go so far as to purposefully sabotage any attempts to apprehend the criminal. They might even cheer quietly to themselves as the masked gunman slipped away under the cover of night.

JOBS THAT AN AWFUL AQUARIUS MIGHT NOT SCREW UP

Clothing designer: Aquarians have a unique sense of style. Sometimes that sense of style is hideous and involves puff paints and bedazzling colours. Other times, however, the Aquarius is able to tap into excellent style combinations and set trends.

Clean up man: If a criminal has a problem, they call a clean-up man or woman. This cleaner descends like a fairy godparent, and gets to work solving the problems at hand. As long as an Aquarius could morally justify the illegality of the work that he or she was doing (maybe by saying that the government was unfairly targeting his or her client), they would love the creative, problem-solving aspect of this job.

Rocket scientist: Aquarius understands the relationship between man-made objects and the physical world more than many other signs. They may teach themselves mathematical and scientific concepts at an early age and their desire to learn knows no bounds. The downside is that an Aquarius in a highly technical field will talk about their job on and on, dropping jargon indiscriminately and openly showing their horror when someone doesn't understand a particular concept.

STARS OF THE SIGN
AWFUL AQUARIUS

Aquarians want to change the world, and those who attempt to do it through their writing do so prolifically. Many notable authors fall under the sign of the Water Bearer and their writing styles are incredibly disparate. Bestselling children's authors include Laura Ingalls Wilder, author of the classic *Little House on the Prairie* series, and Judy Blume, who penned the famous line "I must, I must, I must increase my bust," in her tween novel *Are You There God, It's Me, Margaret*. These works have both been a moral inspiration for young women, as their Aquarian authors no-doubt intended. Fellow Aquarian and Victorian author Charles Dickens penned his most effective social commentaries in the mid-1800s, and deep cultural critiques can also be found in fantasy writer Lewis Carroll's work from the same era. Carroll's novel *Alice's Adventures in Wonderland* is held in high esteem by both children and adults, and has carved out a unique niche for this type of metaphorical commentary. Nearly fifty years after Carroll was tripping out with a rabbit wearing a tuxedo and a caterpillar smoking a hookah, Aquarian authors Virginia Woolf and James Joyce penned their most famous works of social criticism.

Most of the time, Aquarians attempt to impact on the world in more direct ways than writing fiction. Many famous activists are Water Bearers, and their intensity and tireless devotion to their personal causes are apparent in their life's work and in their ability to dampen a party faster than a mouse on the cheese plate. The famous Susan B. Anthony and Harriet Stanton Blatch both dedicated their careers to securing more rights for women, and—of course—Abraham Lincoln was both a very passionate activist for civil rights and a famous drag at social occasions. Aquarian musicians and showbiz stars often use their platform to bring about change, which only adds to the stereotype of celebrities acting like liberal fools. Musician Peter Gabriel is a humanitarian who works with Amnesty International, and Backstreet Boy Nick Carter campaigns for environmental change. Actress Linda Blair is an animal rights activist, while Geena Davis fights for women's rights. Talk show hosts Oprah Winfrey and Ellen DeGeneres are both active with many different charities, so if you get an invitation to a party from any of these people, don't be so starstruck that you don't realize they only want you for your donation to their cause.

Lastly, some clever Aquarians pour their energy into learning about how the world works, and studying science. World-changing scientists Charles Darwin, Thomas Edison, and Galileo were all Aquarians that made incredible professional achievements and yet led puzzling personal lives. For example, Darwin, whose study of biology could easily have informed him of the drawbacks, married his first cousin, Emma. This was not a loveless marriage: the couple produced ten children. Edison married a sixteen-year-old, who worked in one of his shops, after knowing her for only a few weeks. Galileo Galilei, channeling the independent spirit of the Water Bearer, absolutely *refused* to settle down and marry his lover (which was a much bigger deal in his day). The famous astrologer fathered three illegitimate daughters, and they took care of him as he grew old.

AWFUL AQUARIUS BIRTHDAYS

CAPRICORN–AQUARIUS CUSP

People born between January 18 and January 22 fall into the Capricorn-Aquarius cusp and may exhibit traits from both signs. If you can envisage the most idealistic and highly strung do-gooder you know, the one that stands on the highest of all soapboxes, and then mix that person with someone who thinks that all other ideas are despicable and idiotic... then congratulations, you've accurately imagined someone born on the Capricorn-Aquarius cusp.

JANUARY 20

Aquarians born on this date are very determined to do things the right way. They see themselves as upstanding citizens and good role models. On January 20, 1982, Ozzy Osbourne made history by biting the head off a bat, and you can bet that January 20th natives were duly horrified. They mumbled to themselves that if *they* were to bite the head of a bat, they would have done it in such a way that the blood wouldn't have splattered—so very messily—all over their shirt.

JANUARY 21

What's the point of doing something if you can't do it perfectly, January 21st-er? You can't stand to leave things unfinished, and certainly cannot handle doing things half-baked. Famous fashion designer Christian Dior shares this birthday, and his single-minded perfectionism produced culturally vital gems such as the A-line skirt and women's suits. The downside of this perfectionism is that it can really make you come across as a dictator, and your colleagues and kids often feel like chopped liver.

JANUARY 22

People born on January 22 are very comfortable with their dark side. They know that without sadness, depression, and negative emotions, the joys of life will be less vibrant. They can batten down the hatches and thoroughly enjoy grief the way others skip through a field of flowers on a spring day.

JANUARY 23

On January 23, 1943, the film *Casablanca* was released. In the movie, Yvonne asks Rick where he's been, and if she can see him that night. He responds that last night was, "so long ago, I don't remember..." and that, "I never make plans that far ahead." This exchange perfectly encapsulates a January 23rd native's feelings about dating—they refuse to be pinned down. Also, the amount of smoking and drinking that goes on in the film is also a pretty close parallel of a January 23rd Aquarian's unhealthy habits.

JANUARY 24

January 24th-ers are living, walking contradictions. They want to be healthy but can't commit to a diet. They want to have close friendships but can't help but compete with and bait their pals. They want to rebel against authority but feel guilty about their potential disobedience. Unfortunately, their feelings of certainty are unlikely to settle down and this is basically a terminal condition. Even on their deathbeds, they'll be debating with themselves whether to lie on their right side or their left side.

⚡ JANUARY 25

Aquarians born on January 25 are up in the clouds and relatively unreliable in affairs of the heart. They want a fantasy romance, a romance that fills all the empty little places in their soul. For example, Alicia Keys, born on this date, describes an ideal affair as, "I'll be the rising Moon after the setting Sun," and, "I'll be the water you need in the desert land..." When people born on this date realize that their love affair won't live up to those standards, they can become despondent. Even through their despair, they will remain incredibly loyal. Singer Etta James waited for her husband while he served a ten-year prison sentence for a drugs conviction, and Virginia Woolf—in her suicide note—wrote to her husband, "If anybody could have saved me it would have been you. Everything has gone from me but the certainty of your goodness."

⚡ JANUARY 26

If January 26th natives are given an inch, they'll take a mile. If they see an opportunity to increase their power, they'll act on it. They don't have a particular need for close friendships, and prefer to keep others at an arm's length until they find the person with whom they want to spend the rest of their life. While some will see these Aquarians as overly ambitious, they do have a strong moral code and will try to make sure they use the power they gain to change the world for the better.

⚡ JANUARY 27

Did all your pants shrink again in the dryer, January 27th-er? That's a bummer. You should really check the settings on that machine. Look, the honest, harsh truth is that if you don't take your health seriously, you will slowly puff up and your health will become a major concern to you. You don't want to have to be airlifted out of your upstairs window by a flight-for-life helicopter, so please figure out how to make a change and stop *literally* sugarcoating the truth about your bad habits.

⚡ JANUARY 28

People born on January 28 have always had things just a little bit rougher than you did. They work just a little bit harder than you work. They feel just a little sadder, and laugh just a little harder. Their entire existence is one big competition with everyone they encounter, and in their own minds, they're always the winner.

⚡ JANUARY 29

Oprah, everyone's favorite talk show host and super-do-gooder celebrity, was born on January 29. Friends of people born on this date should expect to get inspiration and insight out of their relationship... and maybe even a huge prize akin to the prizes awarded to Oprah's audience members. Not only are January 29th Aquarians very generous with their friends, they also get a great deal of pleasure out of sharing what they've learned about the world. This sounds great, but in reality there's nothing worse than sitting down to a beer with a pal who's trying to inject you with unwanted insight.

⚡ JANUARY 30

January 30th natives are born politicians. They seem accessible, traditional, and aristocratic to the public. To their family, they are demanding and detached and known to stray romantically. And, as in Vice President Dick Cheney's case (he who was born on this date), they might *accidentally* shoot you in the face with birdshot pellets if they don't like what you have to say. Franklin D. Roosevelt was also born on this date, and while he never shot anyone in the face, he did have a long-term affair with his wife Eleanor's social secretary. Roosevelt, in typical Aquarius style, turned his struggle with polio into a cause and established the March of Dimes.

⚡ JANUARY 31

Poor, rich little Aquarius. Because you are good at so many things, you find it difficult to settle on a career. Jackie Robinson, for example, was born on this day. Robinson was a trailblazer, the first African-American Major League Baseball player, and he also excelled at football and track-and-field events, and helped to establish the Freedom National Bank in Harlem. Justin Timberlake shares this birth date and has had rave reviews as a musician, dancer, movie actor, and even as a hot-dog-shaped, singing mascot on *Saturday Night Live*. January 31st native, if you can narrow down your wealth of talents and focus on just one of them, you can be successful. And please let it be as a hot-dog-shaped, singing mascot.

⚡ FEBRUARY 1

Speaking of Justin Timberlake (see above), on February 1, 2004, Justin performed with Janet Jackson at the halftime show of Super Bowl XXXVIII and ripped her costume, exposing her breast on live television. This burst of inappropriate sexuality caused a huge controversy and ended up costing loads of money in fines from the FCC. Like the "wardrobe malfunction" that caused so much trouble, Aquarians born on this date like to be rebellious and defiant, but are horrified and infuriated by the ensuing social consequences of their behavior.

⚡ FEBRUARY 2

Independence at all costs, eh, February 2nd native? If you were born on this day, you protect your autonomy like a mother bear protects her cubs. The second that a job or a significant other begins to make unfair demands on your time or your sovereignty, you head straight to *Splitsville*. Rather than seeing your detachment as a problem, you embrace it. It's only when you start to face those eventual health problems, as you age, that you'll start to wonder why you burned all the bridges you ever crossed.

⚡ FEBRUARY 3

On February 3, 1959, a tragic plane crash killed rock 'n' roll stars Buddy Holly, Ritchie Valens, and J.P. "The Big Bopper" Richardson, Jr. This was a big blow to rock n' roll, and was dubbed "The Day the Music Died," by singer Don McLean. For Richardson this fate was particularly unlucky, not only because he was killed in the oh-so-dull state of Iowa, but because he "won" his seat on the plane through a coin-toss with the guy who was originally supposed to be in the seat. People born on February 3 find themselves with just this sort of ironic, twisted luck. They could find out they've gotten a promotion at work—only to discover that their workload has also tripled. Or they could win some money and have their car promptly break down, with repairs costing more than the winnings. They can't get a winning hand without strings or conditions being attached.

⚡ FEBRUARY 4

Most romances follow a set track: you meet someone, get to know them, and then fall in love with everything you adore about that person. For February 4th natives, it's a totally different experience. They meet someone, fall in love almost at first sight, and then struggle to get to know their lover... and they do not always like what they see, but it's too late. They're already in love and emotionally bonded to the other person. All they can do is just hope that the other person falls *out* of love with them, or simply mysteriously vanishes one day.

⚡ FEBRUARY 5

On February 5 in the year 62 A.D., an earthquake shook the tiny island of Pompeii. This earthquake was the first of several giant, earth-shaking omens that led up to the eruption—seventeen years later—that buried the entire city and all its residents under layers of smoldering ash. People born on February 5th should learn a lesson from the ill-fated residents of Pompeii—take heed of the warnings that come before the fall. If things feel a little bit off at work, check in with your boss and try to avoid a layoff. If your spouse comes home smelling of a cologne or perfume that you don't wear, hire a private eye. Staying on top of the cautionary warnings in your life will help you to avoid the ultimate disasters.

⚡ FEBRUARY 6

People born on February 6 have a story that they present the world about their life. Since they're very charming, no one questions them on their story. The truth is, they take great liberty when they describe where they came from and what propelled them from event to event on their life's timeline. It's not because they are immoral or compulsive liars—they just can't stand a boring back-story.

⚡ FEBRUARY 7

The obsession that people born on this date feel about their work is not just something you can write off with the overused cliché of the "workaholic." February 7th natives *are* their work, or at least they would be happy to be, given the chance. They define themselves through what they study or what they do professionally, and completely integrate their work life with their home life. They do particularly well by professionally championing bleeding-heart causes and don't even care that all their peers are making much more money than they are.

⚡ FEBRUARY 8

February 8th-ers are very content to spend time alone. In fact, when they spend time with other people, they can experience a great deal of social anxiety. They sometimes visualize themselves as the life of the party, but then, when they find themselves around others, they can't seem to find the words to express themselves, and don't convey the same levels of wit and charisma as they do in their own minds.

FEBRUARY 9

It wouldn't even cross a February 9th native's mind to stay in a loveless relationship. They don't believe that love should be a great deal of work, so they might bury a marriage prematurely or walk out on a relationship that has a great deal of potential to make them happy.

FEBRUARY 10

Something's always not quite right with a February 10th-er. They always imagine that they're gaining weight and go on a diet, or they imagine that their hearing is going and go to see the doctor. Maybe their tummy is a little off so they stop eating gluten, wheat, soy, and dairy, and then talk openly about the changes in their stools with anyone who will listen. They're not exactly hypochondriacs, just hyper-aware of their physical bodies and the changes they experience in them.

FEBRUARY 11

People born on February 11 were very charming and precocious children. They maybe even entertained their family's friends with a song-and-dance routine or knock-knock jokes. When they reach adulthood, they realize that they've outgrown the social leniency that comes with being adorable and young, and begin to seek out the approval of sexual partners. They may go through quite a few lovers in their early adulthood and settle down only after establishing their career.

FEBRUARY 12

There's something about February 12th natives that gives them a little bit too much confidence on the dating scene. They think that they can take home anybody from the dance floor. At weddings, they may flirt with the bride and groom. At funerals, they may make eyes with the deceased's remaining spouse. They may feel as though they've been bestowed with a God-given charisma or some psychic force that draws other people to them. This may give them some trouble being faithful in their relationships. But who are they to deny their God-given gifts?

⚡ FEBRUARY 13

People born on February 13 are bound to win even though the odds were all stacked against them. Well, even if the odds aren't all stacked against them, they are still bound and determined. And when they *do* win through vigorous work and cunning smarts (or just dumb luck) they celebrate big-time. They give a toast like no one else and it's not uncommon for them to drink "celebratory" drinks and smoke "celebratory" cigarettes every night of the week.

⚡ FEBRUARY 14

People born on Valentine's Day, February 14, are essentially in big trouble. Health-wise they'll probably develop nervous disorders and relieve their stress through overindulgence in food, cigarettes and alcohol. Money-wise, they'll spend everything they have—and more—with no regard for keeping a budget. Love-wise, they'll actually probably be OK. So that's something.

⚡ FEBRUARY 15

Though eccentric and bearing a mean and sarcastic streak, February 15th natives can find a happy center in their lives through creative careers. The problem is... they're slightly *too* creative and will find themselves bouncing back and forth between projects and unable to complete tasks and move forward. To be truly successful, they need either a super-organized personal assistant, or a spouse who doesn't mind acting like one.

⚡ FEBRUARY 16

Other than the fact that you share your birthday with the late North Korean dictator Kim Jong-Il, there's nothing really wrong with a February 16th birthday. You might be a bit of a perfectionist and have a tendency to require a mental and physical break just as the work gets really hard. Oh yeah, and also, when the North Korean government finds out that you tried to steal their ruler's date of birth, they'll totally annihilate you.

⚡ FEBRUARY 17

Whether they call it God or fate or the Universe at work, people born on February 17 often believe that there's a plan in the works. Because they see themselves almost as a pawn in the grand scheme of things, they rarely get too upset about anything that happens. If they go through a break-up, they imagine it's so that they can meet the person they're supposed to be with. If they run up their credit card debt, it's so that they wouldn't be able to afford the plane ticket on the plane that crashes. While others may find their logic completely-and-utterly illogical, they appreciate the freedom it affords people born on this day.

⚡ FEBRUARY 18

This day generates people with serious star power. There are almost too many stars to mention, but here goes: John Travolta, Dane Cook, Matt Dillon, Jillian Michaels, Yoko Ono, Toni Morrison, Molly Ringwald,

Cybill Shepherd, Vanna White, and Dr. Dre. There are very likely many other swell February 18th natives as well. The reason for their success is simple: they chase after challenges. They not only overcome them with gusto, but they literally attempt the impossible and conquer it. They're voracious and want everything the world has to offer.

⚡ AQUARIUS–PISCES CUSP

If you were born between February 18th and February 23, you fall into the Aquarius-Pisces cusp and may display characteristics from both of the signs. In the case of the Aquarius-Pisces cusp, you may find yourself dismayed when your dreams aren't easily transformed into reality. You have creative, artistic ideas but may lack the know-how or talent to sculpt your vision. When this disappointment hits, your Piscean tendency to become listless and morose may surface, limiting your achievements even further.

PLAGUED PISCES

FEBRUARY 19 TO MARCH 20

No one understands a Pisces... not *really*. If you are born under this rather fishy sign, you can accumulate friends and lovers, be close to your family, seek out a meaningful career, and yet still feel sickeningly alone most of the time. As a Pisces, you have automatically contracted a case of the human condition on steroids and can feel extremely insecure when you encounter life's contradictions and injustices. There is little comfort from the constant churn of Piscean emotions and the sheer weight of your inner tumult makes you a perpetual underdog.

It's not that you don't know the difference between right and wrong. You know the difference, you just refuse to choose. You let the people around you steer your life, so the caliber of people around you determines whether you will end up in jail or on easy street. Since Pisceans aren't always the best judges of character, you might not even be able to see when your entourage is headed up shit creek, but if they say paddle, you'll keep paddling.

281

Pisces feel that they've gotten a raw deal in life, and they're mostly right. They're starting out handicapped because they're paralyzed by their own confusion, depression, and faulty intuition. For other signs who are trying to understand the Piscean experience, just imagine wearing headphones that are screaming constant, conflicting advice, and that you have little bitty alligator arms that prevent you from doing anything for yourself. Those who are high-achieving usually had someone (probably a Virgo or an Aries) kick their ass all the way to the top.

Pisces have a few things going for them, despite their many impediments. One thing is that they're incredibly tuned in to the psychic side. You shouldn't be surprised if a Pisces "knows things" before you tell them. They're sensitive and feel others' losses, absorbing the sadness and carrying it around in their own heart-shaped basket. It's a trade-off, though, because while they carry others' pain, they also expect that others will do things for them, such as forgive them for negligent behavior and support them financially. Sometimes they get lucky and find a partner willing to be in an extended, codependent relationship, but it is not unusual to find a Pisces sitting in the dark alone, drinking away their consciousness, because a loved one didn't do "their part" in this cosmic bargain that the Pisces feels he or she deserves.

LOVE AND RELATIONSHIPS WITH PLAGUED PISCES

Meeting a Pisces for the first time can feel like a fairy tale. Pisces men will sweep you off your feet, wine and dine you, and charm you with their good looks and sweet intellect. Pisces women will be flirty and funny, and unveil their clever, intoxicating charisma as they get to know you. It's almost as if they cast a spell, or set a trap for unsuspecting lovers. After several dates, once their prey is safely ensnared, they begin to reveal their true selves. The magic façade falls away little by little until it's clear that your Pisces is inherently a lazy, miserable soul. With few exceptions, no amount of cajoling or inspirational heart-to-hearts can motivate a Pisces to display genuine ambition, although sometimes they'll go through the motions to placate those around them.

When they're in steady romantic or familial relationships, Pisces can make tolerable companions. Their sensitivity is both their allure and their undoing. They are usually dreamy and creative, which will lead to interesting conversations when they're in the mood to talk. They are good people to have around during a crisis because they are willing to provide comfort to others in pain. They are the friend or lover that would walk thirty minutes uphill in the snow—both ways—to bring you chicken soup when you are sick. And they'd keep doing so every day until you got better. They'd do this mainly because it would give them an excuse to get out of work or other obligations, and that is probably not a good thing in the long run, so try not to encourage their acts of selflessness too often.

Piscean behavior can change in an instant. They are subject to fits of jealousy and they're big mind gamers. If you share your secrets with them, they'll use your own vulnerabilities against you when you argue. Pisces will suck up every bit of attention, affection, intimacy, and passion you have, and it might still not be enough to keep them content in the relationship. Pisces can be unfaithful when they feel disappointed, and have a tendency to screw everything up just when they should be settling down and enjoying their relationship. They may even blame their partner for the infidelity, citing every single romantic failing of the entire relationship.

Being with a Pisces should be a conscious decision, like traveling to a foreign land to knowingly adopt a toddler with emotional problems. The partner needs to be all-in, and needs to take full responsibility for the relationship and its trajectory, even though Pisces will do everything in his or her power to knock it off course. If you, dear reader, decide to go forth and date a Pisces, it might make sense to examine what happened in your childhood to really understand why you feel the need to punish yourself in such a way.

CHECKLIST FOR DATING A PLAGUED PISCES

You'll need at least half of these things in order to have a successful relationship with a Pisces.

Willpower: On the first few dates with your Pisces, you will be charmed by their thoughtfulness and want to jump right into bed and into a relationship with them. It takes willpower to resist the Piscean chemistry. You don't need to resist for ever, just long enough to kick them out, make up the bed, and evaluate the relationship without emotion.

Significant "us" time: You have to be able to be physically and/or emotionally present with your Pisces so that they don't feel neglected. You can't put Pisces in the corner.

Pants: Because you'll be wearing them in the relationship. Pisces crave structure and alpha behavior in their significant others. If you work really hard, you might be able to potty train them, too.

Private detective: You'll need to snoop on your Pisces from time to time, because they tend to be elusive and sneaky. They don't want to lay all their cards out on the table, but this mysteriousness can become a problem when the stakes are high.

Decisiveness: Making decisions upsets Pisces deeply, so don't put them through it. If you can lay out their clothes in the morning, pour their cereal for them, plan their schedule, and handle their social life, both you and your Pisces will be better off.

Prescription drugs: Can you get your hands on some Paxil? Xanax? Zoloft? Yes, yes, and yes. Stock up and distribute antidepressants and antianxiety meds as required.

PLAGUED PISCES COMPATIBILITY

PISCES AND ARIES LOVE

Aries will suck Pisces dry. If the two are a good match, Pisces will enjoy feeling like they're in a game of follow-the-leader. If it's not a good match, Aries will feel like they are the parent of a surly teenager with a crappy attitude.

PISCES AND TAURUS LOVE

The best-case scenario for this couple is if Pisces is a stay-at-home spouse or parent, and Taurus goes out into the world to bring home the bacon. If you try to do it the other way around, you might feel like you're struggling each day to keep things going. Taurus shouldn't feel bad; Pisces was faking any career ambitions they had early on in the relationship.

PISCES AND GEMINI LOVE

Everything seems good at the beginning of a Pisces-Gemini match. The couple will enjoy learning from one another and doing activities or arts-and-crafts together. Then Gemini will say something without thinking and Pisces will mope for the rest of the day. If Gemini can just continue on, undeterred, they might finish the craft and not add it to their growing collection of unfinished projects.

PISCES AND CANCER LOVE

Don't do it. It's such a depressing combination. Cancer pouts even more than Pisces, and both require exhausting levels of emotional engagement from the other. This is a spiral chain reaction of angst just waiting to go off, like a sad line of broken dominos.

PISCES AND LEO LOVE

This relationship could be like when you put multiple Transformer toys together to make one enormous mega-Transformer. The Leo brings the social strength and confidence, and the Pisces brings the humility, and together they somehow turn each other into reasonable people.

PISCES AND VIRGO LOVE

Pisces is to Virgo what a broken leg is to a professional athlete. It will slow them down, diminish their career, and upset them, but they still have a very good chance of surviving the injury.

PISCES AND LIBRA LOVE

In a Pisces-Libra match, it's highly likely that one of you will get friend-zoned quickly. If the relationship continues past the buddy stage, there could be lots of romance to come. Possibly also lots of fights about credit card debt.

PISCES AND SCORPIO LOVE

Scorpio should really think long and hard before entering into a relationship with an unsteady and weak-willed Pisces. The relationship will always be inequitable and Pisces is prone to depression and other mental health issues. If Scorpio is impatient, this match will feel like a lot of unrewarding work.

PISCES AND SAGITTARIUS LOVE

These two should open a small craft beer company, or an Etsy store. If Sagittarius can treat Pisces like a business partner instead of a lover, the two could go places together. On the other hand, if they don't have a mutual goal to shoot for, these two could sit around and blame each other for their shortcomings all day long.

PISCES AND CAPRICORN LOVE

Capricorn has a vision of what they want in their household. They know how it should look and what goes where. If Pisces starts getting potato chip crumbs all over the place, or fails to put kitchen utensils in the right drawer, there could be a lot of bickering. If Pisces gets on board, though, all manner of things could be well.

PISCES AND AQUARIUS LOVE

Imagine a relationship where you don't talk for days or weeks at a time, and you resent each other's very existence. This will be ninety percent of a Pisces-Aquarius match. The remaining ten percent feels so good that the couple foolishly continues to pursue the relationship.

PISCES AND PISCES LOVE

Pisces meets Pisces. This is a slightly disgusting combination because these two will never leave the bedroom. Even when they age out of the pursuit of new and interesting ways to utilize the headboard, they will still just lay around together all day dreaming the same dreams.

CAREER AND MONEY FOR PLAGUED PISCES

First of all, unless a Pisces is very lucky and has a parent or lover pulling their puppet strings, chances are they won't have a particularly rewarding career. In school the fish flounders. The details bog them down, and they get depressed about the work ethic it requires to get over the learning curve. Even the most intelligent Pisces—*especially* the most intelligent Pisces—think they're too cool for school. They have high hopes of structuring their own learning program but lose focus as they begin new projects. If they find a mentor, they might be able to stop from dropping out or otherwise blowing their educational opportunities.

If you're an employer and the resumé of a Pisces comes across your desk, immediately be wary. You do not want this person in your workplace. They won't show up on time, they won't complete tasks by the agreed deadline—but even worse, they won't tell you what's going on so you can help them fix it. Instead of honestly taking an inventory and evaluating what they need to do to be a valuable asset, they'll blame their failures on anything and everything. You might even hear the classically immature, "My dog ate it." Save yourself time and the potential "wrongful termination"

lawsuit by just crumpling up the resumé and placing it in the circular file.

The Pisces who are able to make it in their careers without bringing their whole company down with them are usually in a field that sees their creativity as an asset. Many Piscean artists and writers are able to build their careers by continuing to create a large body of work without paying attention to the haters. They work well alone, in a vacuum, and get overwhelmed if they have to do too much group work. If a Pisces gets too much constructive criticism, they can shut down entirely and spend months or years in a professional funk. Pisces truly believe that they deserve to feel fulfilled in their careers, and even Pisces who have menial or depressingly repetitive jobs will try to connect the job to their inner creativity. If they can succeed in this, they will be able to tolerate their work. Otherwise, they should quickly find the next sugar daddy or mama to take care of them.

ABSOLUTE WORST JOBS FOR A PLAGUED PISCES

Elementary School Teacher: Most of an elementary school teacher's job is a perfect fit for a Pisces. The role allows them to be creative, connect with other people on an intellectual plane, and use their empathy to help guide others. The problem is that they have to show up on time and can't take many days off, and if they're late, a room full of unattended second-graders will eat all the glue or go all *Lord of the Flies* on each other.

Politician: It's unlikely that Pisces hasn't done anything yet to ruin a potential political career. There's some arrest record for petty theft, some addiction that they're struggling with, or—at the very least—some inappropriate sexts they once sent that will come back and haunt them. Plus, being a politician means you have to be in a good mood around large groups people all the time. That's an overwhelming proposition for a fishy Pisces.

Judge: The education and career process of becoming a judge naturally prevents most Pisceans from pursuing it. This is good because Pisceans reliably make the worst decisions in the zodiac, and to elect one as a judge means that anarchy and chaos would soon ensue.

JOBS THAT A PLAGUED PISCES MIGHT NOT SCREW UP

Archive Librarian: If they can manage to show up on time, a Pisces would make a decent archive librarian. Picture a basement filled with shelves and shelves full of dusty books and a lone Pisces soaking up all the knowledge. As long as they don't have to interact with others, they'll probably do this job very well.

Illustrator or graphic artist: Pisces are naturally drawn to the arts, and if they have the motivation to actually finish their pieces and find the right buyers, they could squeak out a living in this field.

Drug dealer: Pisces should consider a career as a drug distribution expert. They are obsessed with the way drugs affect the human body and, as long as they don't oversample the goods, they could create a wonderful lifestyle with the money they make selling drugs.

STARS OF THE SIGN PLAGUED PISCES

Most Pisces are happy just quietly sucking energy from everyone around them. Others really have to go big, and use their Piscean traits to bring about epic destruction. For example, Osama bin Laden was a Pisces. While this should be more than enough to go on, there are many other examples of Pisces that couldn't get past their negative emotions and decided to take their wrath out on everyone around them. James Earl Ray (the man who assassinated Martin Luther King, Jr.) was a Pisces, as is Aileen Wuornos, a prostitute who murdered men along highways in 1989 and 1990.

Not all Pisces goes mad, though. Some Pisces are content to pursue their artistic talents, but it takes a big third-party boost for a Pisces to take off as an artist. Piscean painter Michelangelo had the Medici family, and Renoir had his friend Jules Le Cœur. Interestingly, both painters eventually lost their patrons, likely because they demonstrated their Piscean tendencies of moping, failing to produce work on time, and being generally disagreeable.

Pisces don't limit themselves to spreading their misery and creativity in the field of fine arts. The star sign also lays claim to famously quirky and moody authors such as John Steinbeck and Victor Hugo, as well as actors with a troubled, drug-addled past such as Drew Barrymore and Rob Lowe. Pisces tend to gravitate toward fields that encourage self-destructive behavior.

PLAGUED PISCES BIRTHDAYS

⚡ AQUARIUS–PISCES CUSP

If you were born between February 18 and February 23, you fall in the Aquarius-Pisces cusp. Aquarians have a lot of friends and value their social life, whereas Pisceans prefer to keep to themselves and actively dislike ninety-eight percent of humanity. This means that when you hang out with your many acquaintances, you can't help but sit there, quietly judging them all. The *douchebags*.

⚡ FEBRUARY 19

The book *The Feminine Mystique* was published on February 19, 1963, and explored women's psychological need for a richer, more fulfilling life. Interestingly, people born on February 19 really can't seem to figure out how to split their attention between work and home. They are either bad parents with good careers or good parents with bad careers.

⚡ FEBRUARY 20

As Paul Simon taught the world, there are fifty ways to leave your lover, and it's vital that you find the right way to leave *immediately*. You have the worst taste in partners. The people you choose to hook up with are not just annoying, they're actually really destructive to you either physically or emotionally—or both. So slip out the back, Jack and make a new plan, Stan, because if you don't get yourself free, you'll spend the rest of your life wondering where you went wrong.

⚡ FEBRUARY 21

On February 21, the first Polaroid camera was introduced, paving the way for Instagram and selfies. February 21st natives often spend their entire lives trying to find their "true selves," and they can paralyze themselves by identifying in others only what they *dislike*. They focus on the negatives and miss the bigger picture.

⚡ FEBRUARY 22

You think you deserve something more fulfilling than a nine-to-five gig, right, February 22nd-er? Something that better fits your unique spirit. Well, so did Steve Irwin, who was born this day. He traveled the world and filmed himself messing with all manner of deadly animals. And then he got killed by a stingray. Moral of the story: be careful what you wish for with regard to your career.

⚡ FEBRUARY 23

Do you feel like it's *Groundhog Day* in your bedroom? You know, that movie with Bill Murray where he wakes up on the same day over and over? Except with you it's the same relationship over and over again. The person you're laying next to changes, but the trajectory of feelings and patterns of behavior stay exactly the same.

⚡ FEBRUARY 24

Honestly, how many times have you considered buying an "As Seen on TV" product that would magically fix some issue you're struggling with? You want to lose twenty pounds in a week, grow thicker, more luxurious hair, and clear up your skin overnight. Small changes in your day-to-day schedule can make a difference in your overall health, but if you rely on quick 'n' instant fixes, you'll find that you just continue to get fatter and uglier because you can't find the miracle you're looking for.

⚡ FEBRUARY 25

On February 25, 1836, Samuel Colt received a patent for a gun you did not have to reload in order to fire multiple times. People born on this day have a tendency to fire their mouth off many times without reloading it in their brain, which leads to them feeling guilt and discomfort after social interactions.

⚡ FEBRUARY 26

You don't have to spend any more money on therapy to solve the riddle of why you're so unhappy. It's your parents' fault. Whatever your DNA donors did or didn't do has so deeply scarred you that you'll never feel truly relaxed around other people. Don't worry, they manufacture prescription drugs for this sort of thing.

⚡ FEBRUARY 27

There's street smarts, there's book smarts, and there's February 27th-native smarts. Those smarts may not allow you to become a rocket scientist, or schmooze your way to the top on a golf course, *but you can* continue to find new and exciting ways to emotionally manipulate the people in your life. Oh well, it's better than having no smarts at all.

⚡ FEBRUARY 28

If you were born on February 28, you tend to be a perfectionist. You keep working on projects, deadlines be damned, until you're totally happy with the final product. Unfortunately for your employers, you are incapable of finding happiness in your own work, regardless of whether others like it or not. You treat your relationships that way, too, as though they are projects that you have to keep tinkering with until you get them *just right*, a tendency that will send most significant others running for the hills.

⚡ FEBRUARY 29

Just because your birthday comes once every four years does not mean that you can act like you're a quarter of your actual age. February 29th-ers feel like they are entitled to indulge in unlimited quirkiness and immature behavior. They'll continue to dress, eat, and act like a child long after they are physically mature. (It's *not* cute.) Time to make the leap and grow up.

⚡ MARCH 1

People born on March 1 are attention-hungry humans. They crave all eyes on them, and from infancy to adulthood they focus on what makes other people look at them the most. Then, in adolescence and adulthood, they work to find their own voice. Their levels of talent vary wildly, so sometimes they're captivating and sometimes you'll want to hit them over the head with a cartoon mallet. Examples of people born on this day include Justin Bieber, Ron Howard, and Ke$ha.

MARCH 2

Chris Rock said, "Men are only as faithful as their options." The Pisces ladies and gentlemen born on March 2 find themselves evaluating their options regularly, sometimes consciously and sometimes subconsciously. They love their partner deeply but can't help but fall prey to other sets of batting eyelashes and whispered sweet words from soft, cherry-like lips. Best to lock March 2 natives in some sort of cage if you plan to maintain a relationship with one.

MARCH 3

Hear no evil, see no evil, speak no evil. That's a March 4th-er's motto. They pretend that the problems in their life don't exist, continue to skate on the thin ice, and when everything blows up in their face, they claim they never saw it coming. This is true in their professional life, but particularly common in dealings with their parents and siblings.

MARCH 4

When everything around you always seems to be falling apart, and all your friends are constantly being awful, and your love life seems adversarial at best... it's probably not a coincidence that you are at the center of it all. You actively choose and create chaos, and everyone else would be better off in the long run if they refused to make eye contact with you from now on.

MARCH 5

Do not trust someone born on March 5 with financial matters. Just don't. They have a knack for avoiding good deals while simultaneously seeking out bad investments. The worst part is that they *think* they're quite clever with money and brag about all the fancy footwork they're doing to put their money to work. The best thing for these March 5th-ers is to take a rudimentary course in balancing one's checkbook. Upon successful completion, maybe award them a weekly allowance.

⚡ MARCH 6

There is a person in your family with whom you're having a feud. The other person probably doesn't know you're having a feud—he or she just thinks you're an odd duck. You, on the other hand, positively seethe about it, and it sometimes keeps you up at night. You think about what you should have said, you think about what you'll say next time, and you go over and over the principles at stake. You chew on this issue like a cow chews cud. If you change your perspective and think of this feud as a hobby, you can really adjust your worldview for the better. Keep a journal, or a scrapbook, of the feud. Plot pranks and set traps at family gatherings. It will be more fun for everyone that way.

⚡ MARCH 7

March 7th Pisceans are delicate creatures with delicate internal systems that they in no way treat in a delicate fashion. Most people born on this day jam their bodies full of prescription drugs, alcohol, nicotine, and everything else they can find to help make them feel good. What they'll never learn is that... if they just stopped doing this, they'd feel a whole lot better.

⚡ MARCH 8

How many times have you switched educational or career paths? The stars report that your dreamy

Piscean nature gets you into trouble because every time a new idea crosses your mind, you want to throw yourself entirely into it. You may have a degree or two, or you might just spend all your time on Internet research, trying to teach yourself how to sew authentic-looking civil war replica costumes. Either way, you skate from one intellectual obsession to the next and this will prevent you from building a satisfying career in any one field.

⚡ MARCH 9

You are what you do, March 9th Pisces. You define yourself through your daily activities, be they work or play oriented, and that identity becomes a sort of veil that you hide behind. You're a "reader" or a "teacher" or a "photographer" or a "kickball player," and once you've picked an identity you spend a lot of energy making sure you get it right. Hmm, what would a kickball player wear to Sunday brunch? Aha! What would a photographer say to the mother of the bride at a wedding? You'll figure it out. And then you'll say it. Because you *are* a photographer... today, anyway.

⚡ MARCH 10

This is actually one of the worst birthdays in the entire zodiac. People born on this day have the emotional control of a toddler. There are just so many angry, unruly March 10th people pulling trains of chaos behind them, and this is evidence enough to prove that there is some malevolent, mysterious swirl of furious energy floating around for these unfortunate Pisces. Chuck Norris found a way to harness this energy to be a badass. Osama bin Laden, international terrorist, and James Earl Ray—Martin Luther King, Jr.'s assassin—

let the anger lead them to horrible acts. If you were born on this day, you carry so much judgment and frustration about others that it can cause you to do terribly destructive things. The thing you struggle to understand is *yes*, the world is imperfect, and *it's OK*. Really, March 10th-er, please get your feelings under control and try not to destroy anything.

⚡ MARCH 11

You really remember your first love. You think about him or her on a regular basis and play the "what if" game, unless of course you're still with your first love. If you're still together, the relationship is probably fairly unpleasant because you idealize how it *should* be and won't settle for anything less. When your partner doesn't live up to this, you can be cruel and unrelenting. If you're not still together, you're a borderline stalker, so ease up. Unless you're just cyberstalking, in which case, carry on.

⚡ MARCH 12

Growing up is hard to do, and your life will be plagued—even more than the lives of all other Pisceans—with romantic unrest and indecision until you mature emotionally. Unfortunately for March 12th natives, this process of maturation requires incredibly hard knocks to ricochet you up to higher emotional levels.

⚡ MARCH 13

You need to find a job that allows you to lose yourself. This birthdate is home to artists, photographers, and burlesque dancers. Those with less artsy careers can also lose themselves in the rhythm and science of whatever they're doing, and can find themselves hypnotized by their work. You are not great at separating work from your personal life, and you probably dream about your job often. Which is totally not fair, because you do not get paid for those hours unless you fib a little on your timesheet.

⚡ MARCH 14

As you may know, you were born on Pi Day. That's the day celebrating the mathematical constant, 3.14—the ratio of a circle's circumference to its diameter. Pi is an irrational number and you are an irrational human. Emotionally irrational, that is. Albert Einstein was born on 3.14 and he was a beacon of intellectual rationality, but his hair is clear evidence of his emotional instability. You, like Einstein, struggle to find a way to be productive while your personal life looms distractingly in the background. Also, like Einstein, you have an inexplicable sexual magnetism.

⚡ MARCH 15

"Beware the Ides of March," said the soothsayer to Julius Caesar. The Ides, or the 15th, of March is the birthdate of people who should be careful when it comes to lofty goals. They set goals based on what would make others around them happy, and are depressed when they continue to fall short of those goals. They don't know of any other way to set goals, so they continue in this cycle of falling short. As Caesar would say, Rome wasn't built in a day, so March 15th natives might want to start with tiny baby steps. Number one: get out of bed today. Number two: put on some pants. That's a good start.

⚡ MARCH 16

On March 16, 1968, American troops—Company C, nicknamed "Charlie"—killed and mutilated nearly 500 Vietnamese villagers. The victims included men, women, children, babies, and animals. This atrocity is impossible to comprehend. This is the kind of thing that keeps people with March 16th birthdays from enjoying their own lives. They can't ignore the injustices of the world like everyone around them can. To them, the glass isn't half-empty or half-full, it is a glass filled with the tears of sweatshop workers on the other side of the globe. In short, March 16th natives are not very fun to have at cocktail parties.

⚡ MARCH 17

The stars have much in store for March 17th natives. They are blessed with brilliance and the ability to work hard and persevere, but cursed with the feeling of never being good enough. Designer Alexander McQueen, who sadly took his own life, is an example of how

Pisceans born on this day can shine on the outside while succumbing to dark thoughts on the inside. John Wayne Gacy, a serial killer known as "The Killer Clown," also embodies some of these traits. If you were born on this day, the more you succeed, the more you will expect of yourself, so it might be best to keep the bar low and stay out of the dark place.

⚡ MARCH 18

Dionysus is the Greek god of wine and of ritual madness and ecstasy. Whenever Dionysus is around, you're sure to find orgies and feasts and drunk people everywhere. People born on March 18 seem to have the Dionysian spirit. They don't tell themselves "no" very often and tend to be promiscuous and overindulge with food and drink. As they get older, they get slightly more predictable... but somehow maintain their insatiable, visceral appetites.

⚡ MARCH 19

Aw! Everyone around you just wants to take care of you. You will seem like a child to others for ever, and evoke warm and fuzzy feelings of affection. Even if you do naughty things, most people will probably just see you as impetuous, not a jackass. It's slightly annoying to you because you see yourself as a little bit of a cowboy, or a free agent that don't need nothin' from nobody. It's adorable when you act like that, so don't stop mentioning how independent you are when you're in social situations. *So cute!*

⚡ MARCH 20

Everyone knows that you have a side that you're not showing the world. Some people want to know more about that side, while others are content with the face you show them. For example, Mr. Rogers (Fred to his closest friends), was born on March 20, and everyone who ever watched him tie his shoes knows that there must be more to that man than meets the eye.

⚡ PISCES—ARIES CUSP

People born March 19 through March 23 fall into the Pisces-Aries cusp. The signs of Pisces and Aries are extremely different. The Pisces is the fish that goes with the flow, and Aries whips out the horns and butts his or her way through when faced with an obstacle. What you get when you combine the two is someone who starts big projects but can't see them through. Someone that talks a big talk but doesn't quite live up to the big promises.